Aries

Dedications

For the memory of Gary Bailey, a new star in heaven.
For the memory of Frances Waxman, who always marched to her own drum beat.

Acknowledgements
We gratefully acknowledge the help given to us by Lynn Beddoe, Claire Champion, Anne Christie, Grant Griffiths and Liz Dean who have all helped enormously with the production of this book.

Aries

Sasha Fenton and Jonathan Dee

This edition published 1996 for Parragon Books
Units 13–17 Avonbridge Industrial Estate
Atlantic Road
Avonmouth, Bristol BS11 9QD
by Diamond Books
77–85 Fulham Palace Road
Hammersmith, London W6 8JB

ISBN 0 75251 901 8

Phototypeset by Intype London Ltd
Printed in Great Britain

Contents

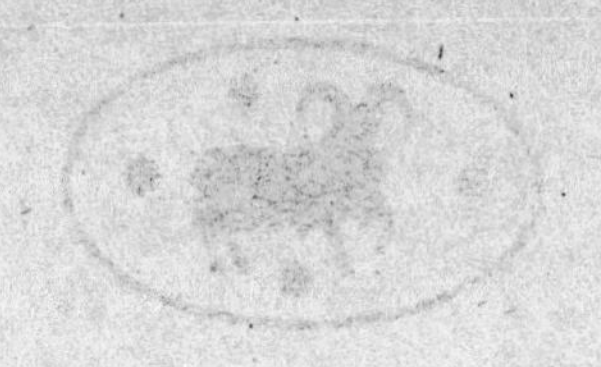

The Essential Aries

YOUR RULING PLANET Your ruling body is Mars. Mars was once the Roman god of War and, as such, has always been seen as aggressive and dynamic. The ancient Greek version is Ares (or Aries), so your sign and ruling planet really do fit well together. The planet Mars has a slightly reddish colour, which probably led the Ancients to associate the planet with the fiery energy of their warrior god.

YOUR SYMBOL Your symbol is the ram. The ram first appeared in ancient Egypt representing the first of the gods, Ammon. This is very apt for the first sign of the zodiac. In ancient times, Aries was also symbolised by the goose, although the origins of this connection have been lost in the mists of time.

PARTS OF THE BODY Aries rules the head, eyes, skull and upper jaw. Ariens are often red-haired when young, and many Aries men can lose their hair in middle age. A mole, scar or other mark on the forehead is quite common. Ariens usually have a small nose and chin, and rather full cheeks.

YOUR GOOD BITS Your best qualities are energy and initiative, a capacity for hard work and a love of life.

YOUR BAD BITS Your worst qualities are selfishness,

impatience, aggression and a dislike of thoroughness.

YOUR WEAKNESSES Fast cars, fast lovers, fast food.

YOUR BEST DAY Tuesday. In ancient times, Tuesday was ascribed to the Roman god Mars, also your ruling planet.

YOUR WORST DAY In theory, Friday is your worst day. This is because it is associated with Venus, a planet that is traditionally different from Mars. However, Ariens usually love 'thank God it's Friday', because the weekend is hard on its heels.

YOUR COLOUR Bright crimson red.

CITIES Birmingham, Florence, Naples, Boston, Sydney.

COUNTRIES England, Germany, Japan, Indonesia.

HOLIDAYS Anywhere where there is plenty to look at and lots of shops. The markets of Bangkok are the Arien's spiritual home.

YOUR FAVOURITE CAR Your favourite auto would be a company car that is provided for you, looked after and paid for by someone else! If you cannot run to that, then a second-hand motor would do, especially if it is slightly unusual in some way.

YOUR FAVOURITE MEAL OUT You love eating out and will enjoy almost any type of food, especially if it is interesting and well presented. However, you probably enjoy dining with your friends and family at home even more than going out to restaurants. Most Ariens are unfussy eaters, but traditional astrology suggest onions, radishes and garlic, or any other food with a sharp flavour.

YOUR FAVOURITE DRINK If you are a drinker, you will probably drink anything that's going. However, most Ariens are very modest drinkers, preferring a spritzer or a drop of wine with a meal when out with friends.

YOUR HERBS Basil, witch hazel.
YOUR TREES Thorn, chestnut.
YOUR FLOWER Honeysuckle.
YOUR ANIMALS Vulture, fox, ostrich, leopard. Also the sheep or ram, of course!
YOUR METAL The metal associated with your sign is iron. Iron has a low melting point and is the metal from which early weapons were made. Oxidised (rusted) iron is a reddish colour.
YOUR GEMS Aries has various associated gems, especially the hard unyielding diamond and the passionate bloodstone.
MODE OF DRESS Anything new! You love buying clothes: your taste may be plain or flamboyant but you love new things. You seek to disguise a large behind.
YOUR CAREERS Any large organisation. Sports, medicine, engineering, teaching, and those that require wearing a uniform are favourites. Ariens make excellent mediums and writers and they also do well in voluntary work.
YOUR FRIENDS Honest, energetic, intelligent and generous people.
YOUR ENEMIES Devious or indecisive types, or penny-pinching nit-pickers.
YOUR FAVOURITE GIFT Ariens love gadgets, so a pocket computer game, an electronic desk game or a new sports car would suit both males and females of the species. Both sexes also love new clothes, so a trip to the shops (preferably on someone else's credit card!) would be very acceptable indeed.
YOUR LUCKY NUMBER Your lucky number is 1. To find your lucky number on a raffle ticket or something similar, first add the number together. For example, if one of your lottery numbers is 28, add 2 + 8 to make 10; then add 1 + 0, to give the root number

of 1. The number 316 on a raffle ticket works in the same way. Add 3 + 1 + 6 to make 10: then add 1 + 0, making 1. As your lucky number *is* 1, multiples such as 1, 10, 100 or 1000 would all work well, as would 91, 181, 271 or any similar combination. A good lottery choice for you would include at least some of these numbers: 1, 10, 19, 28, 37 and 46.

Your Sun Sign

Taurus

Ruled by Mars

21st March to 20th April

Yours is a masculine, fire sign and your symbol is the ram. This combination gives you courage, a love of adventure and travel, plus energy, initiative and a determination to live life to the full.

Impulsive, enterprising, energetic, self-centred, pioneering, courageous, generous, highly-sexed . . . does this fit you? Well, some of it probably does but there are other, rather different sides to your personality. For instance, you love your home and, whether it is a complete tip or a palace, it is *yours* and nobody is going to take it away from you. You like your family and you are probably quite happy in your marriage or partnership. Some Ariens get off on the wrong foot in partnerships, admit failure and bring the relationship to an end. But having done so, they go on to choose more wisely the second time around and really work to make a go of things. Some of you hang on to outworn relationships, probably due to possessive feelings about those things which you once owned. Some of you cling to your children long after they should have left the nest, while others would love your kids to be off your hands but find it difficult to get them out of the house and out of your hair and, oh boy, how they love scrounging money from you!

Ariens of both sexes can fall madly in love and then drive yourselves, not to mention your friends, completely crazy while you extol the virtues of your beloved or wonder aloud for the umpteenth time, 'just where is this relationship going?' Although you love the early and exciting stages of a courtship, you are happier and more relaxed when in something more comfortable and enduring. Sex is an important part of any relationship for you and you will not stay with a partner for long if this is denied you. Some Ariens are happy to have plenty of straightforward lovemaking, while others can be real fantasisers.

You are competitive as well as somewhat impulsive but you don't take chances where it matters. For example, you may slog away in a fairly uninspiring job, doing your best and working as part of a team, but pit all your real energy and competitiveness against others in a sporting activity or a hobby. Many Ariens become professional sports people. This is partly due to competitiveness, but also because of your terrific energy-bank. You are happy to work in a large organisation or at the head of a team, and many of you seem to wind up in jobs that require specialised clothing or hard hats.

You are extremely sociable and fond of eating out with a drink or two to go with it. At any kind of function, you can be seen hopping and bopping and flirting like mad with anyone who catches your eye. You can't take too much sitting around indoors and you need something to look forward to at weekends. You are happy to spend money on entertainments but you can be surprisingly stingy about other things, especially the kind of mundane household or family expense that prompts you to ask, 'do you *really* want that, dear?'

One really typical Arien peculiarity is your behaviour towards visitors. You welcome them with a drink, biscuit and anything else they may need and then, just when they are comfortable and ready for a good old gossip, you walk out of the room, leaving them sitting there!

All the Other Sun Signs

Taurus

21st April to 21st May

These people are practical and persevering. Taureans are solid and reliable, regular in habits, sometimes a bit wet behind the ears and stubborn as mules. Their love of money and the comfort it can bring may make them very materialistic in outlook. They are most suited to a practical career which brings with it few surprises and plenty of money. However, they have a strong artistic streak which can be expressed in work, hobbies and interests.

Some Taureans are quick and clever, highly amusing and quite outrageous in appearance, but underneath this crazy exterior is a background of true talent and very hard work. This type may be a touch arrogant. Other Taureans hate to be rushed or hassled, preferring to work quietly and thoroughly at their own pace. They take relationships very seriously and make safe and reliable partners. They may keep their worries to themselves but they are not usually liars or sexually untrustworthy.

Being so very sensual as well as patient, these people make excellent lovers. Their biggest downfall comes later in life when they have a tendency to plonk themselves down in front of the television night after night, tuning out the rest of the world. Another problem with some Taureans is their 'pet hate', which they'll harp on about at any given opportunity. Their virtues are common sense, loyalty, responsibility and a pleasant, non-hostile approach to others Taureans are much brighter than anyone gives them credit, and it is hard to beat them in an argument because they usually know what they are talking about. If a Taurean is on your side, they make wonderful friends and comfortable and capable colleagues.

Gemini

22nd May to 21st June

Geminis are often accused of being short on intellect and unable to stick to anyone or anything for long. In a nutshell, great fun at a party but totally unreliable. This is unfair: nobody works harder, is more reliable or capable than Geminis when they put their mind to a task, especially if there is a chance of making large sums of money! Unfortunately, they have a low boredom threshold and they can drift away from something or someone when it no longer interests them. They like to be busy, with plenty of variety in their lives and the opportunity to communicate with others. Their forte lies in the communications industry where they shamelessly pinch ideas and improve on them. Many Geminis are highly ambitious people who won't allow anything or anyone to stand in their way.

They are surprisingly constant in relationships, often marrying for life but, if it doesn't work out, they will walk out and put the experience behind them. Geminis need relationships and if one fails, they will soon start looking for the next. Faithfulness is another story, however, because the famous Gemini curiosity can lead to any number of adventures. Geminis educate their children well while neglecting to see whether they have a clean shirt. The house is full of books, videos, televisions, CDs, newspapers and magazines and there is a phone in every room as well as in the car, the loo and the Gemini lady's handbag.

Cancer

22nd June to 23rd July

Cancerians look for security on the one hand and adventure and novelty on the other. They are popular because they really listen to what others are saying. Their own voices are attractive too. They are naturals for sales work and in any kind of advisory capacity. Where their own problems are concerned, they can disappear inside themselves and brood, which makes it hard for others to understand them. Cancerians spend a good deal of time worrying about their families and, even more so, about money. They appear soft but are very hard to influence.

Many Cancerians are small traders and many more work in teaching or the caring professions. They have a feel for history, perhaps collecting historical mementoes, and their memories are excellent. They need to have a home but they love to travel away from it, being happy in the knowledge that it is there waiting for them to come back to. There are a few Cancerians who seem to drift through life and expect other members of their family to keep them.

Romantically, they prefer to be settled and they fear being alone. A marriage would need to be really bad before they consider leaving, and if they do, they soon look for a new partner. These people can be scoundrels in business because they hate parting with money once they have their hands on it. However, their charm and intelligence usually manage to get them out of trouble.

Leo

24th July to 23rd August

Leos can be marvellous company or a complete pain in the neck. Under normal circumstances, they are warm-hearted, generous, sociable and popular but they can be very moody and irritable when under pressure or under the weather. Leos put their heart and soul into whatever they are doing and they can work like demons for a while. However, they cannot keep up the pace for long and they need to get away, zonk out on the sofa and take frequent holidays. These people always appear confident and they look like true winners, but their confidence can suddenly evaporate, leaving them unsure and unhappy with their efforts. They are extremely sensitive to hurt and they cannot take ridicule or even very much teasing.

Leos are proud. They have very high standards in all that they do and most have great integrity and honesty, but there are some who are complete and utter crooks. These people can stand on their dignity and be very snobbish. Their arrogance can become insufferable and they can take their powers of leadership into the realms of bossiness. They are convinced that they should be in charge and they can be very obstinate. Some Leos love the status and lifestyle which proclaims their successes. Many work in glamour professions such as the airline and entertainment industries. Others spend their day communing with computers and other high-tech gadgetry. In loving relationships, they are loyal but only while the magic lasts. If boredom sets in, they often start looking around for fresh fields. They are the most generous and loving of people and they need to play affectionately. Leos are kind, charming and they live life to the full.

Virgo

24th August to 23rd September

Virgos are highly intelligent, interested in everything and everyone and happy to be busy with many jobs and hobbies. Many have some kind of specialised knowledge and most are good with their hands, but their nit-picking ways can infuriate colleagues. They find it hard to discuss their innermost feelings and this can make them hard to understand. In many ways, they are happier doing something practical than dealing with relationships. Virgos can also overdo the self-sacrificial bit and make themselves martyrs to other people's impractical lifestyles. They are willing to fit in with whatever is going on and can adjust to most things, but they mustn't neglect their own needs.

Although excellent communicators and wonderfully witty conversationalists, Virgos prefer to express their deepest feelings by actions rather than words. Most avoid touching all but very close friends and family members and many find lovey-dovey behaviour embarrassing. They can be very highly sexed and may use this as a way of expressing love. Virgos are criticised a good deal as children and are often made to feel unwelcome in their childhood homes. In turn, they become very critical of others and they can use this in order to wound.

Many Virgos overcome inhibitions by taking up acting, music, cookery or sports. Acting is particularly common to this sign because it allows them to put aside their fears and take on the mantle of someone quite different. They are shy and slow to make friends but when they do accept someone, they are the loyalest, gentlest and kindest of companions. They are great company and have a wonderful sense of humour.

Libra

24th September to 23rd October

Librans have a deceptive appearance, looking soft but being tough and quite selfish underneath. Astrological tradition tells us that this sign is dedicated to marriage, but a high proportion of them prefer to remain single, particularly when a difficult relationship comes to an end. These people are great to tell secrets to because they never listen to anything properly and promptly forget whatever is said. The confusion between their desire to co-operate with others and the need for self-expression is even more evident when at work. The best job is one where they are a part of an organisation but able to take responsibility and make their own decisions.

While some Librans are shy and lacking in confidence, others are strong and determined with definite leadership qualities. All need to find a job that entails dealing with others and which does not wear out their delicate nerves. All Librans are charming, sophisticated and diplomatic, but can be confusing for others. All have a strong sense of justice and fair play but most haven't the strength to take on a determinedly lame duck. They project an image which is attractive, chosen to represent their sense of status and refinement. Being inclined to experiment sexually, they are not the most faithful of partners and even goody-goody Librans are terrible flirts.

Scorpio

24th October to 22nd November

Reliable, resourceful and enduring, Scorpios seem to be the strong men and women of the zodiac. But are they really? They can be nasty at times, dishing out what they see as the truth, no matter how unwelcome. Their own feelings are sensitive and they are easily hurt, but they won't show any hurt or weakness in themselves to others. When they are very low or unhappy, this turns inwards, attacking their immune systems and making them ill. However, they have great resilience and they bounce back time and again from the most awful ailments.

Nobody needs to love and be loved more than a Scorpio, but their partners must stand up to them because they will give anyone they don't respect a very hard time indeed. They are the most loyal and honest of companions, both in personal relationships and at work. One reason for this is their hatred of change or uncertainty. Scorpios enjoy being the power behind the throne with someone else occupying the hot seat. This way, they can quietly manipulate everyone, set one against another and get exactly what they want from the situation.

Scorpios' voices are their best feature, often low, well-modulated and cultured and these wonderful voices are used to the full in pleasant persuasion. These people are neither as highly sexed nor as difficult as most astrology books make out, but they do have their passions (even if these are not always for sex itself) and they like to be thought of as sexy. They love to shock and to appear slightly dangerous, but they also make kind-hearted and loyal friends, superb hosts and gentle people who are often very fond of animals. Great people when they are not being cruel, stingy or devious!

Sagittarius

23rd November to 21st December

Sagittarians are great company because they are interested in everything and everyone. Broad-minded and lacking in prejudice, they are fascinated by even the strangest of people. With their optimism and humour, they are often the life and soul of the party, while they are in a good mood. They can become quite down-hearted, crabby and awkward on occasion, but not usually for long. They can be hurtful to others because they cannot resist speaking what they see as the truth, even if it causes embarrassment. However, their tactlessness is usually innocent and they have no desire to hurt.

Sagittarians need an unconventional lifestyle, preferably one which allows them to travel. They cannot be cooped up in a cramped environment and they need to meet new people and to explore a variety of ideas during their day's work. Money is not their god – they will work for a pittance if they feel inspired by the task. Their values are spiritual rather than material. Many are attracted to the spiritual side of life and may be interested in the Church, philosophy, astrology and other New Age subjects. Higher education and legal matters attract them because these subjects expand and explore intellectual boundaries. Long-lived relationships may not appeal because they need to feel free and unfettered, but they can do well with a self-sufficient and independent partner. Despite all this intellectualism and need for freedom, Sagittarians have a deep need to be cuddled and touched and they need to be supported emotionally.

Capricorn

22nd December to 20th January

Capricorns are patient, realistic and responsible and they take life seriously. They need security but they may find this difficult to achieve. Many live on a treadmill of work, simply to pay the bills and feed the kids. They will never shun family responsibilities, even caring for distant relatives if this becomes necessary. However, they can play the martyr while doing so. These people hate coarseness, they are easily embarrassed and they hate to annoy anyone. Capricorns believe fervently in keeping the peace in their families. This doesn't mean that they cannot stand up for themselves, indeed they know how to get their own way and they won't be bullied. They are adept at using charm to get around prickly people.

Capricorns are ambitious, hard working, patient and status-conscious and they will work their way steadily towards the top in any organisation. If they run their own businesses, they need a partner with more pizazz to deal with sales and marketing for them while they keep an eye on the books. Their nit-picking habits can infuriate others and some have a tendency to 'know best' and not to listen. These people work at their hobbies with the same kind of dedication that they put into everything else. They are faithful and reliable in relationships and it takes a great deal to make them stray. If a relationship breaks up, they take a long time to get over it. They may marry very early or delay it until middle age when they are less shy. As an earth sign, Capricorns are highly sexed but they need to be in a relationship where they can relax and gain confidence. Their best attribute is their genuine kindness and their wonderfully dry, witty sense of humour.

Aquarius

21st January to 19th February

Clever, friendly, kind and humane, Aquarians are the easiest people to make friends with but probably the hardest to really know. They are often more comfortable with acquaintances than with those who are close to them.

Being dutiful, they would never let a member of their family go without their basic requirements, but they can be strangely, even deliberately, blind to their underlying needs and real feelings. They are more comfortable with causes and their idealistic ideas than with the day-to-day routine of family life. Their homes may reflect this lack of interest by being rather messy, although there are other Aquarians who are almost clinically house proud.

Their opinions are formed early in life and are firmly fixed. Being patient with people, they make good teachers and are, themselves, always willing to learn something new. But are they willing to go out and earn a living? Some are, many are not. These people can be extremely eccentric in the way they dress or the way they live. They make a point of being 'different' and they can actually feel very unsettled and uneasy if made to conform, even outwardly. Their restless, sceptical minds mean that they need an alternative kind of lifestyle which stretches them mentally.

In relationships, they are surprisingly constant and faithful and they only stray when they know in their hearts that there is no longer anything to be gained from staying put. Aquarians are often very attached to the first real commitment in their lives and they can even re-marry a previously divorced partner. Their sexuality fluctuates, perhaps peaking for some years then pushed aside while something else occupies their energies, then high again. Many Aquarians are extremely highly sexed and very clever and active in bed.

Pisces

20th February to 20th March

This idealistic, dreamy, kind and impractical sign needs a lot of understanding. They have a fractured personality which has so many sides and so many moods that they probably don't even understand themselves. Nobody is more kind, thoughtful and caring, but they have a tendency to drift away from people and responsibilities. When the going gets rough, they get going! Being creative, clever and resourceful, these people can achieve a great deal and really reach the top, but few of them do. Some Pisceans have a self-destruct button which they press before reaching their goal. Others do achieve success and the motivating force behind this essentially spiritual and mystical sign is often *money.* Many Pisceans feel insecure, most suffer some experience of poverty at some time in their early lives and they grow into adulthood determined that they will never feel that kind of uncertainty again.

Pisceans are at home in any kind of creative or caring career. Many can be found in teaching, nursing and the arts. Some find life hard and are often unhappy; many have to make tremendous sacrifices on behalf of others. This may be a pattern which repeats itself from childhood, where the message is that the Piscean's needs always come last. These people can be stubborn, awkward, selfish and quite nasty when a friendship or relationship goes sour. This is because, despite their basically kind and gentle personality, there is a side which needs to be in charge of any relationship. Pisceans make extremely faithful partners as long as the romance doesn't evaporate and their partners treat them well. Problems occur if they are mistreated or rejected, if they become bored or restless or if their alcohol intake climbs over the danger level. The Piscean lover is a sexual fantasist, so in this sphere of life anything can happen!

You and Yours

What is it like to bring up an Arien child? What kind of father does an Aquarian make? How does it feel to grow up with a Scorpio mother? Whatever your own sign is, how do you appear to your parents and how do you behave towards your children?

The Aries Father

Arien men take the duties of fatherhood very seriously. They read to their children, take them on educational trips and expose them to art and music from an early age. They can push their children too hard or tyrannise the sensitive ones. The Aries father wants his children not only to *have* what he didn't have but also to *be* what he isn't. He respects those children who are high achievers and who can stand up to him.

The Aries Mother

Arien women love their children dearly and will make amazing sacrifices for them, but don't expect them to give up their jobs or their outside interests for motherhood.

Competitive herself, this mother wants her children to be the best and she may push them too hard. However, she is kind-hearted, affectionate and not likely to over-discipline them. She treats her offspring as adults and is well loved in return.

The Aries Child

Arien children are hard to ignore. Lively, noisy and demanding, they try to enjoy every moment of their childhood. Despite this, they lack confidence and need reassurance. Often clever but lacking in self-discipline, they need to be made to attend school each day and to do their homework. Active and competitive, these children excel in sports, dancing or learning to play a pop music instrument.

The Taurus Father

This man cares deeply for his children and wants the best for them, but he doesn't expect the impossible. He may lay the law down and he can be unsympathetic to the attitudes and interests of a new generation. He may frighten young children by shouting at them. Being a responsible parent, he offers a secure family base but he may find it hard to let them go when they want to leave.

The Taurus Mother

These women make good mothers due to their highly domesticated nature. Some are real earth mothers, baking bread and making wonderful toys and games for their children. Sane and sensible but not highly imaginative, they do best with a child who has ordinary needs and they get confused by those who are 'special' in any way. Taurean mothers are very loving but they use reasonable discipline when necessary.

The Taurus Child

Taurean children can be surprisingly demanding. Their loud voices and stubborn natures can be irritating. Plump, sturdy and strong, some are shy and retiring, while others can bully weaker children. Artistic, sensual and often musical, these children can lose themselves in creative or beautiful hobbies. They need to be encouraged to share and express love and also to avoid too many sweet foods.

The Gemini Father

Gemini fathers are fairly laid back in their approach and, while they cope well with fatherhood, they can become bored with home life and try to escape from their duties. Some are so absorbed with work that they hardly see their offspring. At home, Gemini fathers will provide books, educational toys and as much computer equipment as the child can use, and they enjoy a family game of tennis.

The Gemini Mother

These mothers can be very pushy because they see education as the road to success. They encourage a child to pursue any interest and will sacrifice time and money for this. They usually have a job outside the home and may rely on other people to do some child minding for them. Their children cannot always count on coming home to a balanced meal, but they can talk to their mothers on any subject.

The Gemini Child

These children needs a lot of reassurance because they often feel like square pegs in round holes. They either do very well at school and incur the wrath of less able children, or they fail dismally and have to make it up later in life. They learn to read early and some have excellent mechanical ability while others excel at sports. They get bored very easily and they can be extremely irritating.

The Cancer Father

A true family man who will happily embrace even step-children as if they were his own. Letting go of the family when they grow up is another matter. Cancerian sulks, moodiness and bouts of childishness can confuse or frighten some children, while his changeable attitude to money can make them unsure of what they should ask for. This father enjoys domesticity and child rearing and he may be happy to swap roles.

The Cancer Mother

Cancerian women are excellent home makers and cheerful and reasonable mothers, as long as they have a part-time job or an interest outside the house. They instinctively know when a child is unhappy and can deal with it in a manner which is both efficient and loving. These women have a reputation for clinging but most are quite realistic when the time comes for their brood to leave the nest.

The Cancer Child

These children are shy, cautious and slow to grow up. They may achieve little at school, 'disappearing' behind louder and more demanding classmates. They can be worriers who complain about every ache and pain or suffer from imaginary fears. They may take on the mother's role in the family, dictating to their sisters and brothers at times. Gentle and loving but moody and secretive, they need a lot of love and encouragement.

The Leo Father

These men can be wonderful fathers as long as they remember that children are not simply small and rather obstreperous adults. Leo fathers like to be involved with their children and encourage them to do well at school. They happily make sacrifices for their children and they truly want them to have the best, but they can be a bit too strict and they may demand too high a standard.

The Leo Mother

Leo mothers are very caring and responsible but they cannot be satisfied with a life of pure domesticity, and need to combine motherhood with a job. These mothers don't fuss about minor details. They're prepared to put up with a certain amount of noise and disruption, but they can be irritable and they may demand too much of their children.

The Leo Child

These children know almost from the day they are born that they are special. They are usually loved and wanted but they are also aware that a lot is expected from them. Leo children appear outgoing but they are surprisingly sensitive and easily hurt. They only seem to wake up to the need to study a day or so after they leave school, but they find a way to make a success of their lives.

The Virgo Father

These men may be embarrassed by open declarations of love and affection and find it hard to give cuddles and reassurance to small children. Yet they love their offspring dearly and will go to any lengths to see that they have the best possible education and outside activities. Virgoan men can become wrapped up in their work, forgetting to spend time relaxing and playing with their children.

The Virgo Mother

Virgoan women try hard to be good mothers because they probably had a poor childhood themselves. They love their children very much and want the best for them but they may be fussy about unnecessary details, such as dirt on the kitchen floor or the state of the children's school books. If they can keep their tensions and longings away from their children, they can be the most kindly and loving parents.

The Virgo Child

Virgoan children are practical and capable and can do very well at school, but they are not always happy. They don't always fit in and they may have difficulty making friends. They may be shy, modest and sensitive and they can find it hard to live up to their own impossibly high standards. Virgoan children don't need harsh discipline, they want approval and will usually respond perfectly well to reasoned argument.

The Libra Father

Libran men mean well, but they may not actually perform that well. They have no great desire to be fathers but welcome their children when they come along. They may slide out of the more irksome tasks by having an absorbing job or a series of equally absorbing hobbies which keep them occupied outside the home. These men do better with older children because they can talk to them.

The Libra Mother

Libran mothers are pleasant and easy-going but some of them are more interested in their looks, their furnishings and their friends than their children. Others are very loving and kind but a bit too soft, which results in their children not respecting them or walking all over them in later life. These mothers enjoy talking to their children and encouraging them to succeed.

The Libra Child

These children are charming and attractive and they have no difficulty in getting on with people. They make just enough effort to get through school and only do the household jobs they cannot dodge. They may drive their parents mad with their demands for the latest gadget or gimmick. However, their common sense, sense of humour and reasonable attitude to life makes harsh discipline unnecessary.

The Scorpio Father

These fathers can be really awful or absolutely wonderful, and there aren't any half-measures. Good Scorpio men provide love and security because they stick closely to their homes and families and are unlikely to do a disappearing act. Difficult ones can be loud and tyrannical. These proud men want their children to be the best.

The Scorpio Mother

These mothers are either wonderful or not really maternal at all, although they try to do their best. If they take to child rearing, they encourage their offspring educationally and in their hobbies. These mothers have no time for whiny or miserable children but they respect outgoing, talented and courageous ones and can cope with a handful.

The Scorpio Child

Scorpio children are very competitive, self-centred and

unwilling to co-operate with brothers, sisters, teachers or anyone else when in an awkward mood. They can be deeply unreadable living in a world of their own and filled with all kinds of strange angry feelings. At other times, they can be delightfully caring companions. They love animals, sports, children's organisations and group activities.

The Sagittarius Father

Sagittarian fathers will give their children all the education they can stand. They happily provide books, equipment and take their offspring out to see anything interesting. They may not always be available to their offspring, but they make up for it by surprising their families with tickets for sporting events or by bringing home a pet for the children. These men are cheerful and childlike themselves.

The Sagittarius Mother

This mother is kind, easy-going and pleasant. She may be very ordinary with suburban standards or she may be unbelievably eccentric, forcing the family to take up strange diets and filling the house with weird and wonderful people. Some opt out of child rearing by finding child minders while others take on other people's children and a host of animals in addition to their own.

The Sagittarius Child

Sagittarian children love animals and the outdoor life but they are just as interested in sitting around and watching the telly as the next child. These children have plenty of friends whom they rush out and visit at every opportunity. Happy and optimistic but highly independent, they cannot be pushed in any direction. Many leave home in late teens in order to travel.

The Capricorn Father

These are true family men who cope with housework and child rearing but they are sometimes too involved in work to spend much time at home. Dutiful and caring, these men are unlikely to run off with a bimbo or to leave their family wanting. However, they can be stuffy or out of touch with the younger generation. They encourage their children to do well and to behave properly.

The Capricorn Mother

Capricorn women make good mothers but they may be inclined to fuss. Being ambitious, they want their children to do well and they teach them to respect teachers, youth leaders and so on. These mothers usually find work outside the home in order to supplement the family income. They are very loving but they can be too keen on discipline and the careful management of pocket money.

The Capricorn Child

Capricorn children are little adults from the day they are born. They don't need much discipline or encouragement to do well at school. Modest and well behaved, they are almost too good to be true. However, they suffer badly with their nerves and can be prone to ailments such as asthma. They need to be taught to let go, have fun and enjoy their childhood. Some are too selfish or ambitious to make friends with other children.

The Aquarian Father

Some Aquarian men have no great desire to be fathers but they make a reasonable job of it when they have to. They cope best when their children are reasonable and intelligent but, if they are not, they tune out and ignore them. Some Aquarians will spend hours inventing games and toys for their children while all of them value education and try to push their children.

The Aquarian Mother

Some of these mothers are too busy putting the world to rights to see what is going on in their own family. However, they are kind, reasonable and keen on education. They may be busy outside the house but they often take their children along with them. They are not fussy homemakers, and are happy to have all the neighbourhood kids in the house. They respect a child's dignity.

The Aquarian Child

These children may be demanding when very young but they become much more reasonable when at school. They are easily bored and need outside interests. They have many friends and may spend more time in other people's homes than in their own. Very stubborn and determined, they make it quite clear from an early age that they intend to do things their own way. These children are likely to suffer from nerves.

The Pisces Father

Piscean men fall into one of two categories. Some are kind and gentle, happy to take their children on outings and to introduce them to art, culture, music or sport. Others are disorganised and unpredictable. The kindly fathers don't always push their children. They encourage their kids to have friends and a pet or two.

The Pisces Mother

Piscean mothers may be lax and absent-minded but they love their children and are usually loved in return. Many are too disorganised to run a perfect household so meals, laundry etc. can be hit and miss, but their children prosper despite this, although many learn to reverse the mother and child roles. These mothers teach their offspring to appreciate animals and the environment.

The Pisces Child

These sensitive children may find life difficult and they can get lost among stronger, more demanding brothers and sisters. They may drive their parents batty with their dreamy attitude and they can make a fuss over nothing. They need a secure and loving home with parents who shield them from harsh reality while encouraging them to develop their imaginative and psychic abilities.

Your Rising Sign

What is a Rising Sign?

Your rising sign is the sign of the zodiac which was climbing up over the eastern horizon the moment you were born. This is not the same as your Sun sign; your Sun sign depends upon your date of birth, but your rising sign depends upon the time of day that you were born, combined with your date and place of birth.

The rising sign modifies your Sun sign character quite considerably, so when you have worked out which is your rising sign, read page 35 to see how it modifies your Sun sign. Then take a deeper look by going back to 'All the Other Sun Signs' on page 8 and read the relevant Sun sign material there to discover more about your ascendant (rising sign) nature.

Can Your Rising Sign Tell You More About Your Future?

When it comes to tracking events, the rising sign is equal in importance to the Sun sign. So, if you want a more accurate forecast when reading newspapers or magazines, you should read the horoscope for your rising sign as well as your Sun sign. In the case of books such as this, you should really treat yourself to two – one to correspond with your rising sign, and another for your usual Sun sign, and read both each day!

One final point is that the sign that is opposite your rising sign (or ascendant) is known as your *descendant.* This shows what you want from other people, and it may give a clue as to your choice of friends, colleagues and lovers (see the chart on page 34). So once you have found your rising sign and read the character interpretation, check out the character reading for your descendant to see what you are looking for in others.

Using the Rising Sign Finder

Please bear in mind that this method is approximate – if you want to be really sure of your rising sign, you should contact an astrologer. However, this system will work with reasonable accuracy wherever you were born, although it is worth checking the Sun and ascendant combination in the following pages and reading the Sun sign character on pages 8–18 for the signs both before and after the rising sign you think is yours. For example, if you think that Capricorn is your rising sign, read the Aries/Sagittarius, Aries/Capricorn and Aries/Aquarius combinations. Then check out the Sun sign character readings for Sagittarius, Capricorn and Aquarius on pages 14, 15 and 16. You will soon see which rising sign fits your personality best.

How to Begin

Read through this section while following the example below. Even if you only have a vague idea of your birth time, you won't find this method difficult; just go for a rough time of birth and then read the Sun sign information for that sign to see if it fits your personality. If you seem to be more like the sign that comes before or after it, then it is likely that you were born a little earlier or later than your assumed time of birth. Don't forget to deduct an hour for summertime births.

1. Look at the illustration below. You will notice that it has the time of day arranged around the outer circle. It looks a bit like a clock face, but it is different because it shows the whole 24-hour day in two-hour blocks.
2. Write the astrological symbol that represents the Sun (a circle with a dot in the middle) in the segment that corresponds to your time of birth. (If you were born during Daylight Saving or British Summer Time, deduct one hour from your birth time.) Our example shows someone who was born between 2 a.m. and 4 a.m.

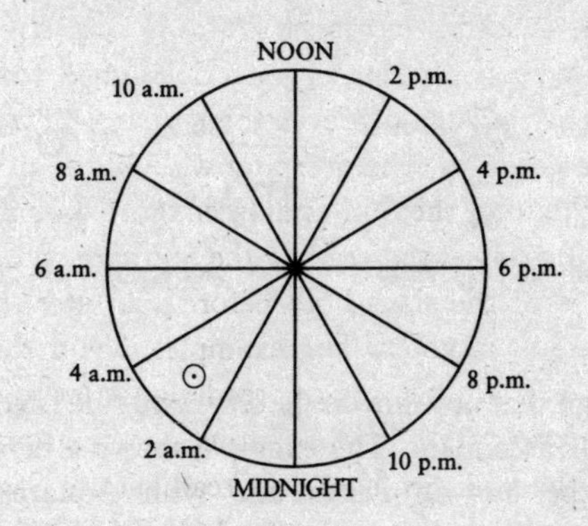

3. Now write the name of your sign or the symbol for your sign on the line which is at the end of the block of time that your Sun falls into. Our example shows a person who was born between 2 a.m. and 4 a.m. under the sign of Pisces.
4. Either write in the names of the zodiac signs or use the symbols in their correct order (see the key overleaf) around the chart in an anti-clockwise direction.

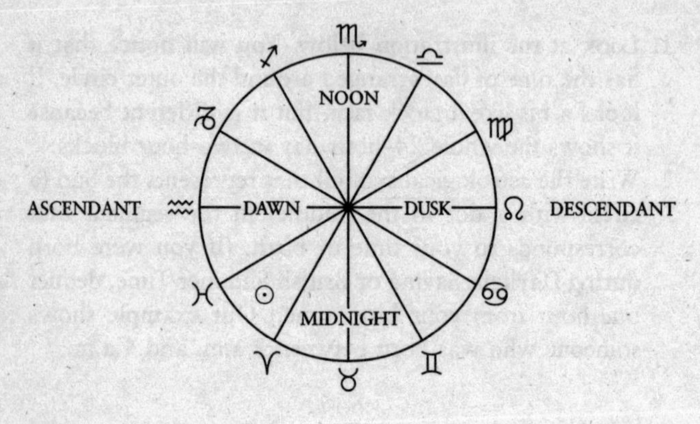

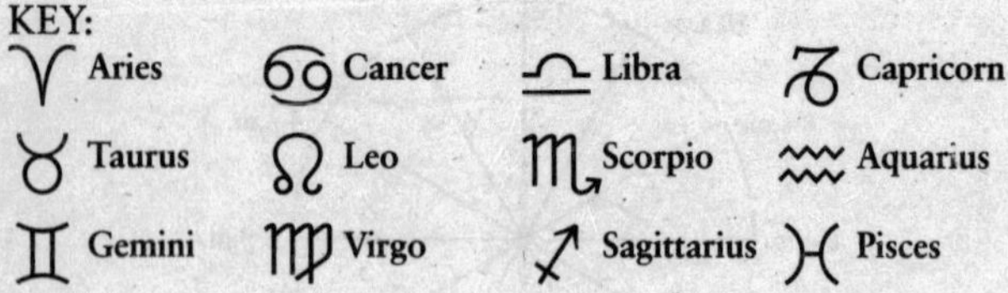

5. The sign that appears on the left-hand side is your rising sign, or ascendant. The example shows a person born with the Sun in Pisces and with Aquarius rising. Incidentally, the example chart also shows Leo in the descendant.

Here is another example for you to run through, just to make sure that you have grasped the idea correctly. This example is for a more awkward time of birth, being exactly on the line between two different blocks of time. This example is for a person with a Capricorn Sun sign who was born at 10 a.m.

1. The Sun is placed exactly on the 10 a.m. line.
2. The sign of Capricorn is placed on the 10 a.m. line.

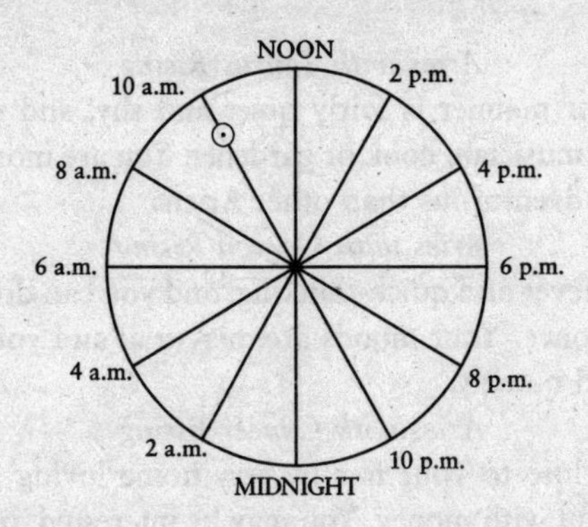

3. All the other signs are placed in astrological order (anti-clockwise) around the chart.

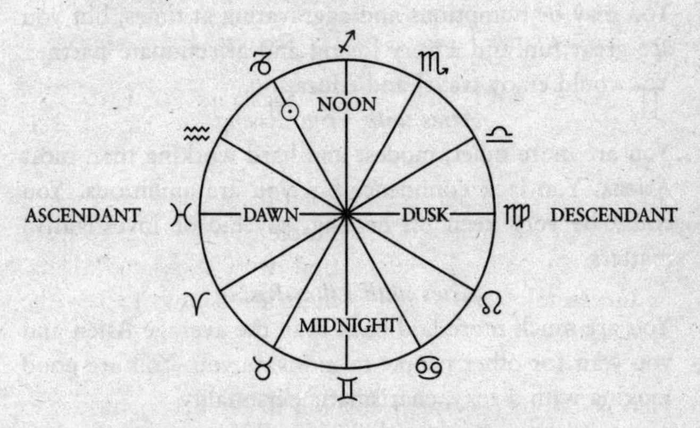

4. This person has the Sun in Capricorn and Pisces rising, and therefore with Virgo on the descendant.

How Your Rising Sign Modifies Your Sun Sign

Aries with Aries Rising

All the Arien traits are strongly marked. If you were born before dawn, you are very outgoing and adventurous, but if you were born after dawn, you will be much quieter, artistic and drawn to mystical or psychic matters.

Aries with Taurus Rising

Your outer manner is fairly quiet and shy, and you may be a keen musician, cook or gardener. You are more settled and less adventurous than other Ariens.

Aries with Gemini Rising

You are clever and quick-thinking, and you can do a dozen things at once. Your moods are mercurial and you change your mind quickly.

Aries with Cancer Rising

You are close to your family, very home loving and also very careful with money. You may be interested in military matters, and attracted to teaching or helping the weak.

Aries with Leo Rising

You may be bumptious and aggravating at times, but you are great fun and a very loving and affectionate partner. You could enjoy travel and education.

Aries with Virgo Rising

You are more quiet, modest and hard working than most Ariens. You lack confidence but you are ambitious. You could be very keen on healing, psychic or investigative matters.

Aries with Libra Rising

You are much more laid back than the average Arien and you wait for other people to motivate you. You are good looking with a sexy, charismatic personality.

Aries with Scorpio Rising

You have a powerhouse personality, being a really hard worker and go-getter who won't let anything stand in your way. The military, police or engineering are areas of work that may attract you.

Aries with Sagittarius Rising

You are a true pioneer, an adventurer with very itchy feet. You could take up a very glamorous job or something wonderful like being a comedian or a top ballet dancer.

Aries with Capricorn Rising

You have a very powerful personality and you want to reach the top, which may compensate you for a difficult childhood.

Aries with Aquarius Rising

You have a funny attitude towards money and goods, possibly amassing them and then giving them away again. You value education and you have a clever, inventive mind.

Aries with Pisces Rising

You may be quiet and shy, but you have strong, self-centred ambition. You could choose an artistic, sporting or glamorous lifestyle.

Aries in Love

You need:

CHEERFULNESS Ariens of both sexes need a cheerful and chatty partner because you dont enjoy sitting around in silence. Your partner must be sociable and happy to make friends with your friends.

PASSION Yours is a highly sexed sign and you need a lover who is as enthusiastic as you are. You need passion in a more general way, in that your partner should have interests or a job that he or she is passionate about. You hate people who are only half alive.

REASON You can't stand sulky or moody people, so your best bet is one who can let a certain amount roll off like water from a ducks back, and who doesn't get into a strop over little things. Real anger for a real reason is something you can understand, especially if your partner is willing to do something about the problem.

You give:

SUPPORT Whether your love is housebound or bound up with a career, you try to help where you can. You will happily take on children, parents and other relatives as well as fixing the car or finding extra money. Both sexes hate housework, and do it because you have to.

SEXUALITY You express your deepest feelings in a loving relationship and can end any argument by making love. You may lack sexual confidence when young, but this improves when you are in a good relationship.

HUMOUR and WIT You could be very clever and you are definitely very amusing. You have a fund of jokes and funny stories and you are good at telling them. You may be a good singer or dancer too. You are entertaining to live with.

What You Can Expect From the Other Zodiac Signs

TAURUS *Security, stability, comfort.* The Taurean will stand by you and try to improve your financial position. They will create a beautiful home and garden for you.

GEMINI *Stimulation, encouragement, variety.* This lover will never bore you; they give encouragement and are always ready for an outing. They give emotional support too.

CANCER *Emotional security, companionship, help.* Cancerians will never leave you stranded at a party or alone when suffering from the flu. They always lend a hand when asked.

LEO *Affection, fun, loyalty.* Leo lovers are very steadfast and they would avenge anyone who hurt one of their family. They enjoy romping and playing affectionate love games.

VIRGO *Clear thinking, kindness, humour.* Virgoans make intelligent and amusing partners. They can be critical but are never unkind. They take their responsibility towards you seriously.

LIBRA *Fair play, sensuality, advice.* Librans will listen to your problems and give balanced and sensible advice. They are wonderfully inventive, and are affectionate lovers too.

SCORPIO *Truth, passion, loyalty.* Scorpios will take your

interests as seriously as they do their own. They will stick by you when the going gets tough and they won't flannel you.

SAGITTARIUS *Honesty, fun, novelty.* These lovers will never bore you and theyll keep up with whatever pace you set. They seek the truth and they don't keep their feelings hidden.

CAPRICORN *Companionship, common sense, laughter.* Capricorns enjoy doing things together and they won't leave you in the lurch when the going gets tough. They can make you laugh too.

AQUARIUS *Stimulation, friendship, sexuality.* Aquarians are friends as well as lovers. They are great fun because you never know what they are going to do next, in or out of bed.

PISCES *Sympathy, support, love.* These romantic lovers never let you down. They can take you with them into their personal fantasy world and they are always ready for a laugh.

Which Sign Are You Compatible With?

Aries/Aries
Too hot for either to handle unless other factors compensate.

Aries/Taurus
Could work if you have interests in common.

Aries/Gemini
Good combination unless the Arien is too bossy or selfish.

Aries/Cancer
Both can be good family members, so this often works well.

Aries/Leo
Unlikely to last long because both want the limelight.

Aries/Virgo
Aries will dominate Virgo until Virgo gets fed up and leaves.
Aries/Libra
A magnetic attraction but often unsuccessful in the long run.
Aries/Scorpio
Very hot and volatile combination but it can work occasionally.
Aries/Sagittarius
Successful, especially where there are shared interests.
Aries/Capricorn
This can work well; Capricorn stabilises the Arien.
Aries/Aquarius
Often very successful because Aquarius ignores Aries' tantrums.
Aries/Pisces
Can work under certain circumstances and with shared interests.

Aries in 1997

Your Year Ahead

Love

If you fall in love right at the beginning of the year, it will be with someone who has influence and a position of honour or status. You won't have to worry about picking up the bills, because your lover will be happy to hand over his or her gold card and pay for your every whim! Well, perhaps it won't be this good, but there is a fair chance that you actually will meet a person of substance this year. If nothing romantic happens at the start of the year, wait for the summer when a chance meeting with a fascinating and very lively person will enhance your life until well after the year's end.

Those of you who are in settled relationships will find yourselves making plans to move into a new property, possibly reaffirming your commitment to each other as part of this. Sex is likely to feature strongly for all Ariens, and this will bring joy and excitement to you on a scale that you have rarely experienced before.

Money

If you get a money-making idea off the ground right at the start of the year, the chances are that you will be able to pursue this to the hilt during the rest of 1997. However, if you are simply trundling along in your usual way, there shouldn't be too much for you to worry about. Friends could come up with a scheme or two, and it is worth listening carefully to their ideas and then perhaps taking one or two of them up. Your financial position is likely to fluctuate quite a bit, with a few really good breaks and also some quite unpleasant setbacks to cope with at times.

Luck

With Saturn in your sign all year, any luck that comes your way will be as a direct result of hard work and a responsible attitude. There should be some lucky breaks in connection with friends or group activities during the first half of the year, but these may have little to do with your career, your home life or your finances. For example, you may be asked to join a prestigious committee or to get involved in a sporting or social activity with a new group of people. Try not to sit around too much this year, because although you are unlikely to win anything big in 1997, it is by being in the swim of things that luck will come your way.

Signs and Symbols

The table at the beginning of each month shows your general trends for the month ahead. The symbols are very easy to understand because the hearts show the state of your love life, the stars tell you how your work is likely to go, the dollar signs tell you whether this will be a good month for money, the heartbeat graphs show your general health and energy levels and the horse shoes tell you whether this will be a lucky month or not.

The Aspects and their Astrological Meanings

CONJUNCT This shows important events which are usually, but not always, good.

SEXTILE Good, particularly for work and mental activity.

SQUARE Difficult, challenging.

TRINE Great for romance, family life and creativity.

OPPOSITE Awkward, depressing, challenging.

INTO This shows when a particular planet enters a new sign of the zodiac, thus setting off a new phase or a new set of circumstances.

DIRECT When a planet resumes normal direct motion.

RETROGRADE When a planet begins to apparently go backwards.

VOID When the Moon makes no aspect to any planet.

January at a Glance

LOVE	♥				
WORK	★	★			
MONEY	$	$	$	$	$
FITNESS	●				
LUCK	∪	∪	∪	∪	∪

Wednesday, 1st January
Moon sextile Pluto

Happy New Year! Communication is the key to relationship success at the start of 1997. Just coasting along because you agree on the little things isn't good enough. So, talk about your beliefs and convictions today and, though you may find differences of opinion, you will reach a deeper understanding of someone who is very important to your future.

Thursday, 2nd January
Sun conjunct Mercury

A free and frank exchange of views is signalled by the conjunction of the Sun and Mercury. In all working situations, from a shop floor conversation to the most high-powered executive meeting, your views are important. Don't hold back. Raise objections to daft schemes, make sensible suggestions for better practices and more advantageous contracts. You can really do yourself some good by being assertive now. If you're unemployed, there couldn't be a better day to arrange or attend interviews.

Friday, 3rd January

Mars into Libra

Today, Mars moves into the area of your chart that is devoted to relationships. This planetary situation is like a double-edged sword, because on the one hand it could bring you closer to your partner or loved one, while on the other hand other people's behaviour could make you extremely angry.

Saturday, 4th January

Moon sextile Sun

You may be faced with a bit of a battle today but your confidence is high and you seem to have an inner conviction that you can win. To be honest, we think that you are quite right!

Sunday, 5th January

Moon sextile Jupiter

Your fast thinking could save the day for someone in a position of authority. This in turn could open a doorway of opportunity for you, so be prepared to take advantage of your boss's goodwill. You could take a stride up the ladder of professional success now simply because you know how to keep a secret.

Monday, 6th January

Mars opposite Saturn

You may be trying like mad to get a new relationship off the ground, only to find that the light of your life is weighed down with work and has only very limited time to spend with you. It is worth making a serious appraisal of the likely passage of this relationship and, if you really cannot see it improving in any way, cut your losses and move on to someone else.

Tuesday, 7th January
Moon conjunct Venus

In total contrast to yesterday's tense aspect, today's stars promise nothing but harmony and contentment. The Moon makes a splendid contact with Venus this Tuesday and bestows the ability to enjoy life to its fullest. Any past family difficulties, such as rows with in-laws, can now be put behind you and oil poured on troubled waters. You'll feel at one with the world.

Wednesday, 8th January
Moon conjunct Mercury

Although the lunar conjunction with Mercury is good news for your verbal self-expression, you could easily get side-tracked by far more interesting things than work. You'll have a grasshopper mind now, so it's very tempting to be more concerned with what other people are doing than getting your head down. You know that you've got a lot on your plate so try to concentrate on the job in hand.

Thursday, 9th January
Jupiter conjunct Neptune

Inspiration and luck combine today as the fortunate planet Jupiter combines with psychic Neptune to give you a lot of insight when dealing with career affairs. When it comes to work problems, follow your instincts because you won't be wrong!

Friday, 10th January
Venus into Capricorn

Venus moves into your solar house of ambition and prominence from today. If you're involved in any career in the arts, beautification, entertainment or public relations then you're bound to do well over the next few weeks. Those who work for women bosses won't do badly either since a female influence in the workplace will aid your ambitions. As Venus is the planet of charisma, use diplomacy to solve professional problems. You can hardly fail to win with such a capacity for charm.

Saturday, 11th January
Venus square Saturn

No matter which way you turn there are demands made on you just now – if it's not one thing it's another. This time it's a combination of your partner and some work worries. You can't seem to still your mind and achieve the inner harmony you so earnestly desire. Try to slow down because you'll be no use to yourself or anybody else if you allow stress to get to you.

Sunday, 12th January
Mercury direct

Mercury returns to direct motion from today and that should put a stop to any disappointments that have bedevilled your career recently. Suddenly, plans you'd put on the back burner are important again. Your path towards your aims will be much smoother than you expect. An ongoing dialogue with an employer or manager will be beneficial to your career prospects.

Monday, 13th January
Moon sextile Sun

Your mood is calm and you seem content to go along with what others want today. Fortunately, others seem to want much the same as you do, so there shouldn't be any conflict of interest now.

Tuesday, 14th January
Moon square Venus

You'd love some quiet relaxation today but some very

well-meaning friends will be determined to drag you kicking and screaming from your shell. It won't matter that you'd like some solitude, or even some intimate time alone with a special person; your friends have decided that the social scene is where you belong. You'll have to be firm about this, because subtle hints won't work.

Wednesday, 15th January
Mercury square Mars

Tempers are frayed in the workplace today. Harsh words may fly as resentments reach boiling point. It's not wise for you to add fuel to this fire because words once spoken cannot be taken back. Try to keep silent to allow the storm to blow over.

Thursday, 16th January
Moon square Uranus

This isn't a day to ask for any favours, especially if they involve money. Those around you are far too negative for their own good, and I'm afraid you're getting some of the fallout. Don't be too impatient, just bide your time. The reason you're likely to be turned down flat today hasn't got anything to do with you really, so try again later in the week.

Friday, 17th January
Sun conjunct Neptune

Other people's problems are the main feature of today. You'll be called upon to provide tea, sympathy and possibly a box of tissues for a friend who needs someone to talk to. Okay, I know you're not the ideal candidate, but take some time out to show that you do care. If work worries or frustrations are at the root of this, at least you'll have an instinctive sense of the way things will go.

Saturday, 18th January
Moon sextile Saturn

Your capacity for hard work, especially mental toil, is awe inspiring today. Your powers of concentration are such that you could easily get through the toughest assignments with ease. Those involved in education will do best from this aspect.

Sunday, 19th January
Sun conjunct Jupiter

All your future hopes are enhanced by today's conjunction between the Sun and Jupiter. The extremely fortunate planetary combination makes this a splendid time for personal enjoyment, happy encounters and pleasure in the company of good friends. Even strokes of bad luck will actually turn out for the best . . . giving a better result than if nothing had happened in the first place. Don't hide your light under a bushel now. The louder you sing your own praises, the more you'll be appreciated.

Monday, 20th January
Sun into Aquarius

As the Sun makes its yearly entrance into your eleventh solar house, you can be sure that friends and acquaintances are going to have a powerful influence on your prospects. The Sun's harmonious angle to your own sign gives an optimism and vitality to your outgoing nature. Social life will increase in importance over the next month. You'll be a popular and much sought-after person. Obstacles that have irritated you will now be swept away.

Tuesday, 21st January
Jupiter into Aquarius

The trials and tribulations of the past few months are fading away rapidly now and you can begin to enjoy the lighter side of life once again. Your sense of humour will come bubbling back up to the surface and there will soon be plenty for you to laugh and joke about. Your best bet is to keep yourself in the swim by joining clubs, societies or groups of people who share your interests.

Wednesday, 22nd January
Mars sextile Pluto

Sudden passions are the order of the day with a strong contact between Mars and Pluto! If you are involved in a close relationship, your other half won't know what's happened to turn you into a wild and wanton love machine. If you are single, then a magnetic personality will attract you.

Thursday, 23rd January
Full Moon

Your creative soul and romantic yearnings come under the influence of today's Full Moon, so it's time to take stock of those things in your life that no longer give any emotional satisfaction. Children and younger people may need a word or two of advice now and the love lives of all around you will become the centre of interest. Your own romantic prospects may see an upturn too.

Friday, 24th January
Sun conjunct Uranus

You're definitely out to make a splash on the social scene right now. As the Sun conjuncts Uranus you're determined to have fun, laugh a lot and, just perhaps, shock a few of your more straight-laced friends. You're certainly full of inventiveness and ingenuity so you can demonstrate the originality needed to enhance your future plans.

Saturday, 25th January

Sun trine Mars

An excellent outlook if you or your partner are interested in sport or other competitive events. A time of fun is forecast in which you will meet many people who share your interests.

Sunday, 26th January

Mars trine Uranus

When you are inspired by an ideal you are a formidable contender, but even you must realise that pooling your energies with a like-minded individual can create an impact that is truly awesome. Get together with those who are as dedicated as you and the sky's the limit.

Monday, 27th January

Moon trine Venus

Your job, career or business is taking precedence just at the moment. This is probably not the time to be terribly creative or experimental in what you are doing, but simply to plod along your usual path and do what you have to do. You may have nothing more exciting than household chores to occupy yourself with now, but these are unavoidable and you might as well do them properly.

Tuesday, 28th January

Moon trine Jupiter

If you and your lover get together with friends, you will find that a chat will do much to cheer you both up and reassure you on one or two points. A visit to your local hostelry might be just the place for this. There should be good news about money matters coming your way today, and the results of this will be shared between you and your lover.

Wednesday, 29th January
Moon square Mercury

Today is the day to visit your doctor if you have any minor ailments or worries. It is a fact that most symptoms disappear as soon as you get to the doctor, but you should look into any ailments anyway, even if only to satisfy yourself that there really isn't much wrong.

Thursday, 30th January
Moon square Neptune

This is going to be a confusing day! Any efforts to help will, in fact, hinder your partner or work colleague. Your suggestions seem to miss the point and are probably impractical. At least your heart's in the right place.

Friday, 31st January
Moon square Uranus

This is a good day to get out and about to meet people. If you don't fancy venturing too far from home you could simply pop in to your local pub or club. There are people to be met, and if you happen to be unattached, a sudden attraction could alter that single state quite rapidly. This is not a time to be on your own.

February at a Glance

LOVE	♥	♥	♥		
WORK	★				
MONEY	$	$	$	$	$
FITNESS	●	●			
LUCK	∪	∪	∪		

Saturday, 1st February
Venus conjunct Neptune

At last, a restful day! You know you could do with one so it's with a sigh of relief that the rays of Venus and Neptune combine to provide an aura of gentle affection. You'll gratefully realise how much someone close has sacrificed to aid your ambitions. Their selfless acts should now be repaid with a demonstration of your love.

Sunday, 2nd February
Moon conjunct Pluto

Your curiosity is stimulated as the Moon contacts Pluto today. Nature abhors a vacuum so you'll be absorbing all sorts of snippets of information now. Try to be selective in your sources otherwise you'll end up as confused as you were in the first place.

Monday, 3rd February
Venus into Aquarius

Venus moves into your eleventh house of friendship and group activities today, bringing a few weeks of happiness and harmony for you and your friends. You could fall in love under this transit or you could reaffirm your feelings towards a current partner. You should be looking and feeling rather good now but if not, this is a good time to spend some money on your appearance and also to do something about any nagging health worries.

Tuesday, 4th February
Moon square Saturn

Red tape, officious authorities and irritating store assistants are all obstacles you'll have to meet with today. Nothing is easy at a time when the Moon is harshly aspected to Saturn. This could be a stellar message advising you to slow down, and rethink your plans. Perhaps you're expecting too much in too short a time. If so, then consider your options again.

Wednesday, 5th February
Uranus sextile Pluto

Today's rare aspect between Uranus and Pluto can't be pinned down to one day or even one week. It provides a revolutionary influence that could affect your life in the most unexpected of ways over the coming months. You have probably been feeling a kind of inner pressure and a strong desire for change. For many of you, this will result in a sudden move, both in your social circle, and possibly in your place of residence. Distant travel will become very appealing.

Thursday, 6th February
Mars retrograde

Mars turns backwards today, and this could have annoying consequences in an established relationship. A quarrelsome atmosphere may prevail for a while. Try not to score points off each other or rise to the bait in any way. Calm and patience are a must now.

Friday, 7th February

New Moon

There's no doubt that issues surrounding friendship and trust are very important now. The New Moon in your horoscopic area of social activities ensures that encounters with interesting people will yield new and enduring friendships. Though your mood has tended to vary between optimism and despondency recently, the New Moon can't fail to increase your confidence and vitality.

Saturday, 8th February

Mercury conjunct Neptune

You're quite likely to be having second thoughts today. The rational processes that are the gift of Mercury are dimmed in the confusing influence of Neptune. You may feel that all your high-flown aims are just too much for you to cope with. Hold your course – you can be sure it's the right thing to do.

Sunday, 9th February

Jupiter sextile Saturn

Good news signalling that one of your wishes is about to come true should arrive today. If you've courted disappointment recently, you should hear that your troubles will soon ease considerably.

Monday, 10th February

Moon conjunct Saturn

Every now and again, you lose your natural optimism and zest for life. That's the case today as the Moon conjuncts Saturn, putting a dampner on your self-image. If you're wise you should avoid dismal people, keep well away from intense films and programmes, and not dwell on any past failures. You need something light and amusing about you to offset the depressive inclinations of the day. Treat yourself well. Eat something you like and wear something colourful.

Tuesday, 11th February
Mercury conjunct Jupiter

The wheel of fortune turns in your favour today with the conjunction of Mercury and Jupiter. Mists have cleared from your vision and you can again see the enormous potential open to you. For many the planetary link will create professional connections with foreign countries. For others there could be the chance of a new, more fulfilling job or a promotion in the offing. This is an excellent day for attending interviews, writing to potential employers and talking over plans with those who can use their influence to advance your schemes.

Wednesday, 12th February
Moon square Neptune

The vague or downright silly attitudes of someone around you may be irritating, but you should tolerate differences with calmness today. It may be that you take a look at your spiritual needs. But each to his own as they say. All the same don't believe everything you're told.

Thursday, 13th February
Mercury conjunct Uranus

Prepare to be surprised or even shocked by some of the statements that spill from the lips of someone you thought you knew well. Amazement like this can only be caused by a conjunction of Mercury and Uranus which shakes up your previously staunch opinions in a challenging way. Good will come of this as you are forced to reassess your position and goals in life.

Friday, 14th February

Jupiter sextile Pluto

If there was any question as to who was the most dominant in your crowd, there'll be no question that it's you from now on! Your complete mastery of any situation will be obvious, and probably appreciated.

Saturday, 15th February

Mars opposite Saturn

A difficult day as far as relationships are concerned. In both business affairs and more personal partnerships the outlook is dodgy. Keep to yourself as much as possible today and don't get drawn into long-running disputes.

Sunday, 16th February

Jupiter conjunct Uranus

A day of surprises when Jupiter and Uranus get together. Unpredictable events in the lives of your friends will have the happiest and most fortunate of outcomes. Laughs and happy events are due today.

Monday, 17th February

Moon square Mars

You're in a crabby, cranky and cantankerous mood today. The folk closest to you had better watch their step if they don't want to risk a temper tantrum. Try to realise that your argumentative state is due to overstrain and tiredness as much as deliberate needling from your kith and kin, and make allowances for yourself.

Tuesday, 18th February

Sun into Pluto

The Sun moves into your house of secrets and psychology today making you realise your own inner world of dreams and imagination. For the next month you'll be very aware of the hurdles that face you, and all those things that tend to restrict your freedom. However, your imagination and almost psychic insight will provide the necessary clues to overcome these obstacles. Issues of privacy are very important over the next few weeks.

Wednesday, 19th February
Saturn trine Pluto

On reflection, you will come to the conclusion that some things in your life have got to change. It may be your image that requires attention, or the way in which you express your personality. It is equally certain that you're the one who has to achieve this transformation.

Thursday, 20th February
Moon opposite Jupiter

Children could cost you money now or they could in some way prevent you from taking up an appealing offer or two. You may be restricted by obligations to your family and you will have to put duty and responsibilities before personal freedom for a while. It is worth letting your friends know how much you value them, because they do help to lift your spirits when they can.

Friday, 21st February
Moon opposite Venus

Your energy level is low at the moment, so don't set yourself a list of tiresome tasks. Just go through the motions while at work. Plan an evening of resting on the sofa, watching your favourite video or chatting idly to your lover. Don't put any demands upon yourself today, get a take-away dinner and glance through the papers until you doze off.

Saturday, 22nd February

Full Moon

Something is coming to a head in relation to your work. This is not a major crisis and there is absolutely no need to flounce out of a perfectly good job, but there is a problem that should be solved before you can continue on in a happy and peaceful frame of mind. You may have to sort out what your role is and which part of the job other people should be doing, because it looks as if you are carrying too much of the load at the moment.

Sunday, 23rd February

Sun square Pluto

It's as if the Sun has decided to force the issue of psychological cleansing by getting into a tussle with Pluto at the start of this week. You're questioning everything! Daily habits, established pathways, cherished beliefs . . . nothing is sacred! You really want to know if you're clinging to outmoded thoughts or practices. One thing is sure; this celestial wrestling match will be worth it, no matter how uncomfortable it is now.

Monday, 24th February

Moon conjunct Mars

Something important concerning relationships must be tackled over the next few weeks. You and your lover will be putting extra energy into your relationship now. This may be in the form of taking up a sporting hobby or some other kind of shared interest now or you may simply decide to see a bit more of each other. Business or working partnerships will benefit from this planetary movement as well.

Tuesday, 25th February

Moon opposite Saturn

You are full of questions today, and some of them aren't easy to answer. Both you and a partner have to ask yourselves where you are going, and whether your emotional link is strong enough to withstand the ups and downs of life. You'll probably find that the answer is 'Of course it is', but you must admit that there are some imperfections. Set your minds to sorting those out and you'll be all right.

Wednesday, 26th February

Moon square Neptune

The lunar aspect to Neptune ensures that this will be a confusing day. You may think that you are acting in the best interests of all those who are around you, but it seems that your sympathy is actually being taken for granted.

Thursday, 27th February

Venus into Pluto

As Venus enters your solar house of secrets and psychology, it's obvious that the next few weeks will increase the importance of discretion in your romantic life. You'll find that it'll be wise to draw a veil over the more intimate side of your nature, and you'll be less inclined to confide your deepest secrets even to your closest friends. Quiet interludes with the one you love will be far more attractive than painting the town red just now.

Friday, 28th February

Mercury into Pluto

You'll find yourself in a more introspective mood for a few weeks because Mercury, planet of the mind enters the most secret and inward looking portion of your horoscope from today. This is the start of a period when you'll want to understand the inner being, your own desires and motivations. Too much of a hectic life will prove a distraction now so go by instinct and seek out solitude when you feel like it.

March at a Glance

LOVE	♥	♥			
WORK	★	★	★	★	
MONEY	$	$	$	$	$
FITNESS	●	●	●	●	
LUCK	∪	∪	∪		

Saturday, 1st March

Saturn sextile Uranus

A new influence enters your life today as Saturn, which has encouraged an inward-looking frame of mind is perked up by a new person in your life, represented by Uranus. Initially, you may think that this new acquaintance is rather strange but you will like him or her when you get to know them better.

Sunday, 2nd March

Moon square Sun

This is not likely to be an easy day. Your anxiety levels will be high and there doesn't seem to be much that you can do about it! It could be that another person is the cause of your worry, if so then you have to realise that everyone has to make their own mistakes in life.

Monday, 3rd March
Venus square Pluto

Though you are often impulsive, every now and again a warning voice sounds in your inner ear preventing you from a downright stupid course of action. That's the way it is today as Venus and Pluto join forces to divert you from the crooked path. The road to hell is said to be paved with good intentions, so it's a good thing you've got enough common sense to recognise when you're taking the wrong turn.

Tuesday, 4th March
Mercury conjunct Venus

Sometimes you find it difficult to express your deepest feelings, but that is not the case today. You may not be able to verbalise your thoughts, but that doesn't stop you writing them down. You can express yourself clearly now, and may even understand the issues better yourself when they are in black and white.

Wednesday, 5th March
Moon conjunct Neptune

Your imagination is enhanced by the lunar conjunction with Neptune today. Though you are full of dreams about the way things could be, this ideal world doesn't really fit into practical reality. Creativity is stimulated but may lack drive or direction.

Thursday, 6th March
Moon conjunct Jupiter

You may be on the receiving end of a windfall today. A friend may whisk you away to interesting places or there could be unexpected good luck of an unusual kind now. You may receive an invitation to travel to new and fascinating places or you may even win a holiday as a prize of some kind. As you can see, this is one of those truly red-letter days in which anything can happen.

Friday, 7th March
Mars into Virgo retrograde

Mars makes a return visit to your area of health and habits to give you another chance to ditch any of those bad little habits that aren't doing you any good at all. Think fitness!

Saturday, 8th March
Pluto retrograde

All the philosophising you've been indulging in for the last couple of days is certainly showing signs of transforming some of your deepest convictions as Pluto takes a backward step today. The planet's presence in your ninth house has given you a taste of things to come, showing the freedom and wealth of experience that awaits you. Of course there are practical matters to be considered now, and you'd do well to deal with the nitty gritty of life over the next few months.

Sunday, 9th March
New Moon eclipse

The eclipse shows that you are beginning to perceive a pattern in your life. All the good times, the trials and tribulations you've experienced have all had their part to play, and now you're just starting to see a grand design in view. I'm not promising that you'll have all the answers but at least the picture will be clearer.

Monday, 10th March
Sun conjunct Mercury

The Sun and Mercury move into close conjunction today which heightens your imagination. It is too easy to get carried away with an idea now or let baseless fears rule your life. You're quite emotional at the moment, so when the light of reason is overwhelmed by your ego, your anxieties come to the fore. Don't be taken in by flights of fancy.

Tuesday, 11th March
Moon square Neptune

You could be rather gullible today and ready to believe anything said to you in your workplace. Promises will turn out to be no more than hot air. Rely on your own resources and don't expect others to fulfil their promises.

Wednesday, 12th March
Moon square Uranus

Friends aren't a very good influence on you at the moment. Though persuasive, you shouldn't listen to all the airy talk about their money and possessions. It's all a boast, as you'd realise if you were in a more practical frame of mind. Unfortunately, you could be tempted into a spot of 'keeping up with the Joneses', which is too expensive for comfort.

Thursday, 13th March
Moon sextile Sun

A mystery will be resolved today and something that you thought you had lost will suddenly turn up. If you have misunderstood someone else's motives, you will now be able to see what has really been behind their strange behaviour.

Friday, 14th March
Moon opposite Pluto

You may have a charitable disposition but this isn't a time to rub in your moral superiority and put everyone else's backs up. It's not often that you are absolutely certain of anything, but today there's an air of conviction about you that's awe inspiring. Make sure that this belief doesn't go too far and turn you into a bit of a fanatic. A good cause is all very well, but keep a sense of balance.

Saturday, 15th March
Moon square Venus

You're in a languid mood at the moment and want to be left alone with your refined thoughts. Unfortunately, your family is extra-demanding, and though you are fond of them, there are times when you need your own space. Your inner sense of rightness could be offended by the brash and pushy attitudes of those around you.

Sunday, 16th March
Mercury into Aries

The movement of Mercury into your own sign signals the start of a period of much clearer thinking for you. You will know where you want to go and what you want to do from now on. It will be quite easy for you to influence others with the brilliance of your ideas and you will also be able to project just the right image. However, do guard against trying to crowd too much into one day!

Monday, 17th March
Sun opposite Mars

It's the men in your life who are in a bad mood today! Stay close to your female friends and relations and keep away from the male sex for the time being. It will be hard to get any sense out of any man today and, if you are in the unfortunate position of having to deal with male employees, tradesmen or workmen, then you have all our sympathy.

Tuesday, 18th March
Moon opposite Neptune

Although you're feeling reasonably secure, the same might not be said for some of your relations. Over-sensitivity and over-reaction are likely now, and try as you might, there'll be some difficulty in calming down family members. Of course, by the end of this trying time you may be overwrought emotionally too. You'll need a peaceful home environment to relax in.

Wednesday, 19th March
Moon opposite Uranus

Since you're a person who is anxious to please, it's a difficult thing to cope with when you can't please one person without offending someone else. If you can't please all the people all the time, it's better to simply please yourself and let those who are determined to be offended find another excuse. Loyalties can be stretched too far sometimes.

Thursday, 20th March
Sun into Aries

The Sun moves into your own sign today bringing with it a lifting of your spirits and a gaining of confidence all round. Your birthday will soon be here and we hope that it will be a good one for you. You may see more of your family than is usual now and there should be some socialising and partying to look forward to. Music belongs to the realm of the Sun, so indulge yourself with a musical treat soon.

Friday, 21st March
Mercury conjunct Saturn

It's a day of deep thought and deliberation when Mercury conjuncts Saturn. It's becoming more obvious that you are a person of many unfulfilled desires, and now you're very anxious to do something about that. However, there's a note of caution entering your thinking, and wisdom is replacing impulse. Be assured that everything you want is possible, but going at it like a bull at a gate isn't going to get you anywhere.

Saturday, 22nd March
Mercury sextile Jupiter

You are in an amazingly sociable frame of mind today. So much so that, if you can't get in touch with your usual friends or relatives, you will find yourself wandering down to your local hostelry in order to see what new and fascinating folk you can find there. Your energy levels will be higher than usual and this could encourage you to have a go at some kind of unaccustomed sport or other activity.

Sunday, 23rd March
Venus into Aries

The luxury-loving planet, Venus, is suggesting that this is a great time to spoil yourself and also to enjoy yourself. So treat yourself to something gorgeous that is for you alone. A new outfit would be a good idea or a few nice-smelling toiletries. Throw a party for your favourite friends and don't look the other way if someone seems to be fancying you.

Monday, 24th March
Full Moon eclipse

Today's eclipse casts a shadow of doubt over a close relationship. Problems that have been simmering under the surface will now come out and have to be faced. It's no good shying away from serious issues because this can be a make-or-break time.

Tuesday, 25th March
Moon opposite Mercury

Love don't come easy, as the song says. Well, not today, anyhow. It is not worth trying to get on good terms with your lover just now, because everything you try to say or do will be misconstrued. Your motives may be the best but your partner will not be in the best of moods, and he or she may be more interested in having a fit of the sulks than in giving you the love and reassurance that you are searching for.

Wednesday, 26th March
Moon square Neptune

You would be wise to keep your tongue in check today. It is likely that a lover or a work colleague is spinning you a line for reasons of their own. Even though you will be sympathetic to a sob story, don't rush to lend assistance. Wait and see first.

Thursday, 27th March
Moon square Jupiter

You may have to put yourself out on behalf of others today, with friends being especially keen to have your help and energy on their side. Don't resent this kind of activity because it will bring some kind of karmic benefit later on when it will be your turn to call on your friends for their support. Your optimistic and positive outlook will help others to climb out of their melancholy moods.

Friday, 28th March
Moon conjunct Pluto

Frivolous people and subjects won't hold your attention on this Good Friday, because youll be delving deep into yourself right now. The true nature of things is the subject that really absorbs your interest. You want answers but realise that they lie within yourself. Whether you have a scientific, philosophical or religious inclination, you've certainly got food for thought.

Saturday, 29th March
Moon trine Venus

You could have a rather nice day in company with in-laws or some other relative of your partner's today. A woman who is vaguely attached to you in this kind of way will turn out to be amusing and interesting company. This person could help you work out how best to go about decorating or changing part of your home or, if you need some help from an experienced cook, she could be the one to come up with the right recipe.

Sunday, 30th March
Sun sextile Uranus

The tried and true path is not the one to follow this Easter Sunday. The Sun's aspect to Uranus brings some unconventional people into your circle. Be open-minded and ready for new influences in your life. Who knows where it could lead? It may be that you can find a short cut you've never thought of before that will lead to considerable personal achievement.

Monday, 31st March
Sun conjunct Saturn

There's no time for flights of fancy today. The Sun conjuncts grim Saturn in your sign showing that a serious and dutiful attitude is the best course for you to follow now. Though the pressures may be heavy, you've got sufficient strength of purpose to carry on to a successful conclusion. Your care of others may have resulted in ignoring your own interests and that's got to be put right immediately. Don't delay, for though it may take some time, you've got to put yourself first for once.

April at a Glance

LOVE	♥	♥	♥	♥	♥
WORK	★	★	★	★	★
MONEY	$	$	$	$	
FITNESS	●	●	●	●	●
LUCK	∪	∪	∪	∪	

Tuesday, 1st April
Mercury into Taurus

All the planets seem to be restless just now since Mercury changes sign today. At least you can get your mind into gear concerning the state of your finances now. Tasks you've been putting off like cancelling useless standing orders, or ensuring you receive the most advantageous interest from your savings will be tackled with ease now.

Wednesday, 2nd April
Sun conjunct Venus

The conjunction of the Sun and Venus in your own sign is the perfect indicator of romance. Charismatic to a fault, you can easily attract anyone who takes your fancy. For many, this is merely going to mean a pleasant flirtation. For others, this could be the start of a lasting romance. However it turns out, this is a most enjoyable period in which your personality will shine.

Thursday, 3rd April

Sun sextile Jupiter

This is a good day on which to take a small gamble. Don't take this too seriously, but a small wager should come up trumps. There may be a windfall of some other kind and another possibility is that a friend may share a piece of good luck or good news with you by taking you out for a drink or a meal. You may book up a trip on an impulse now or you may decide to get involved in a New Age subject like astrology or the Tarot.

Friday, 4th April

Moon sextile Mercury

Keep a few matters to yourself today. Even if a friend or a neighbour tries to worm things out of you, try to keep your mouth firmly shut. Your financial position is improving rapidly now but it would be a good idea to keep this information to yourself because there are plenty of people around you who would be only too happy to relieve you of any extra pennies that you may have put by.

Saturday, 5th April

Moon opposite Mars

Your mood is dreamy and distant today. You want to disconnect yourself from the world and all its demands and responsibilities. Unfortunately, an opposition between the Moon and Mars in the work sector of your chart today will make this impossible to achieve. Keep your nose to the grindstone, your shoulder to the wheel and put your best foot forward. Later in the day, you can lay whatever is left of your body down for a nice rest.

Sunday, 6th April

Moon trine Pluto

Your mind isn't on practicalities just now, for your

imagination has been caught by the more spiritual aspects of life. Religious and philosophical beliefs are very important to you and you'd like someone to talk things over with. Perhaps a future plan for an educational course should be pursued while you're in this frame of mind.

Monday, 7th April
New Moon

There's a New Moon in your own sign. This is a powerfully positive influence that encourages you to make a new start. Personal opportunities are about to change your life. You must now be prepared to leave the past behind to embark on a brand new course. Decide what you want, because you'll be your own best guide.

Tuesday, 8th April
Mercury square Uranus

Anything could happen today, and we're afraid that the chances are that anything that *does* happen will be disturbing! Disquieting news could come your way, but don't be too ready to believe it.

Wednesday, 9th April
Moon trine Mercury

It's a good day for making solid progress on the career front. You can project an image of someone who gets things done. Your efforts will find favour with those who are important. Those of you who are out of a job may find that an opportunity occurring today will solve your problems.

Thursday, 10th April
Moon trine Neptune

Though today brings a good aspect between the Moon and Neptune your financial situation is prone to deceptive influences. This is not a day when you should be prepared to sign on the dotted line, because you'll be too vague to take much notice of the small print. More generally, you will have a sense of the rightness of your professional course.

Friday, 11th April

Moon trine Jupiter

You will have chatted to so many people by the end of today that your voice will probably be hoarse. All your friends will phone you up, neighbours will stop you in the street, relatives whom you don't talk to from one year's end to another will come round to see you and gossip will flow in and out from all quarters. There will be great news in the post and even your local paper will have something special in it just for you.

Saturday, 12th April

Moon sextile Venus

You're particularly charming and seductive today. You could use your wiles to get your own way in anything, as there are few with enough mental resistance to turn you down flat! You'll be the centre of attention. Affection will be shown to you and you'll be left in no doubt that all around you regard you with fondness and respect.

Sunday, 13th April

Moon sextile Mercury

One of your sisters or brothers or a close friend of around your own generation could have some very good news to pass on to you today. This could be in connection with money or it may be something to do with property or premises. If you have any dealings with partners or colleagues that involve money or possessions, this too should go well today.

Monday, 14th April
Moon square Sun

It's a difficult day emotionally simply because you feel a sense of unease that's hard to pin down. The outlook isn't improved by the harsh lunar aspect to the Sun, which sets your nerves on edge and gives a restlessness that's hard for you, or indeed anyone else to live with. Your own four walls are pressing in. You need some space so get out and about. Relatives, especially older females will tend to irritate by not giving you any credit for intelligence.

Tuesday, 15th April
Mercury retrograde

It's typical – just as Mercury is getting to grips with your financial state, today the wayward planet backtracks sending all cash affairs into chaos. However, this is a temporary problem; just take extra trouble to be completely clear in financial matters right now. Check all facts and figures thoroughly just to be on the safe side.

Wednesday, 16th April
Venus into Taurus

After yesterday's glitch, your financial state should experience a welcome boost for a few weeks as Venus, one of the planetary indicators of wealth, moves into your solar house of possessions and economic security from today. You feel that you deserve a lifestyle full of luxury, and that'll be reflected in the good taste you express when making purchases for your home. Your sense of self-worth is boosted too, which might indicate a renewed interest in high fashion.

Thursday, 17th April
Moon trine Sun

You're in the right mood to enjoy life to the absolute full

today. The Moon splendidly aspects the Sun which enables you to find humour in the most ordinary circumstances. You should get the chance to indulge yourself in a favourite hobby, the more creative the better. For those of a romantic turn of mind, today should present the opportunity for a wonderful amorous liaison.

Friday, 18th April
Moon trine Mercury

There should be great news today, especially in connection with your career. If you are looking for a new job now, you should soon hear just the news you need. There is an upturn in matters related to health as well and, whether it is you or some other member of your circle who has been under the weather, the news for the future is really good.

Saturday, 19th April
Sun square Neptune

You'll be too dreamy for mundane practicalities today. Your idle fantasies could make you look at the world through rose-coloured spectacles. This is okay in your own time, but if you lose your concentration at work, expect a ticking off!

Sunday, 20th April
Sun into Taurus

Your financial prospects take an upturn from today as the Sun enters your house of money and possessions. The next month should see an improvement in your economic security. It may be that you need to lay plans to ensure maximum profit now. Don't expect any swift returns for investments, but lay down a pattern for future growth. Sensible monetary decisions made now will pay off in a big way.

Monday, 21st April

Mercury square Uranus

It won't be wise to lend any money today, no matter how well you know the borrower. Unexpected events will occur that will prevent any sum from being repaid. So solve the problem before it starts and don't part with cash in the first place.

Tuesday, 22nd April

Full Moon

The Full Moon brings to the surface intense feelings that you have buried away in some vault of memory. You'll be forced to look at yourself stripped bare of illusions now. That's not such a bad thing, because you'll realise that many of your hang-ups have been a total waste of time and should be ditched. You may have a financial worry coming to a head, so today's Full Moon encourages you to take the necessary decisive action to sort it out once and for all.

Wednesday, 23rd April

Venus square Uranus

Overspending on luxuries is a distinct possibility today. Your taste may be refined and you love expensive toys, but the depth of your pocket isn't limitless. Leave the credit cards at home!

Thursday, 24th April

Moon square Jupiter

You'll be prone to rather rapid mood swings today. The harsh lunar aspect to Jupiter either makes you overly optimistic or liable to be let down by a close friend. Keep your feet on the ground.

Friday, 25th April
Sun conjunct Mercury

This is an excellent day in which to pull off a really spectacular deal so, if you feel like wheeling and dealing in the big league, then do so now! Even if you are only looking around for something for yourself or your family, you should be able to find just what you want. This is also a good time for buying or selling a vehicle, or for having one repaired.

Saturday, 26th April
Moon sextile Jupiter

If a friend suggests a short holiday, weekend break or just a jaunt to your local shopping centre you should immediately accept. This is your chance to have a lot of fun and encounter some new faces. You will find stimulation in even the most mundane of places!

Sunday, 27th April
Mars direct

Life should be somewhat easier from now on since Mars returns to his more normal direct motion from today. If you've been tired and listless, then this more positive state of affairs should get you back into a vital, go-getting physical and mental state. Equally, if the drudgery of your day-to-day life has had a similar negative effect then you'll find that your enthusiasm and interest in the world around you is renewed.

Monday, 28th April
Sun square Uranus

The negative solar aspect to Uranus warns you to keep a tight grip on your purse strings. Don't be taken in by talk of get-rich-quick schemes or apparently sure-fire investments.

Leave your money where it is . . . in the bank! Don't leave friends in charge of your property, either.

Tuesday, 29th April
Moon square Mercury

A friend may tell you something that upsets you today while another friend may do something that costs you money. With friends like these, do you really need enemies? Your mind is not working at its best now, so don't agree to anything or do anything that you are unsure about. Wait until your judgement is back to full strength.

Wednesday, 30th April
Venus trine Mars

It's not often that anyone finds out just how much their colleagues think of them, but that's your good fortune today. It's a flattering outlook and you may even find that someone at work is romantically interested.

May at a Glance

LOVE	♥	♥	♥	♥	
WORK	★	★	★	★	★
MONEY	$	$	$		
FITNESS	●	●	●	●	●
LUCK	∪	∪			

Thursday, 1st May

Neptune retrograde

Your mind won't be on work for a while since something has got you dreaming of better times to come. The trouble is that while you are fantasising, you won't be doing anything else! Your dreams could possibly come true if you work at achieving them.

Friday, 2nd May

Venus square Jupiter

If a friend asks you for a loan today, think twice. The chances of you getting the money back are probably small but that doesn't mean you shouldn't help your friend. Perhaps it would be better to make an outright gift – maybe of an amount which is smaller than the one asked for – rather than lending money. The laws of karma suggest that any such gift will be returned, although probably in a roundabout way and not from the person to whom it was given.

Saturday, 3rd May

Mercury square Neptune

It's definitely going to be a confusing day when Mercury is in hard aspect to misty Neptune. Since Mercury governs the thought processes, the vague, bewildering influence of Neptune seems to pack your mind in cotton wool. It's not the best day for making financial commitments, or indeed entering any important agreements at all. Don't make big decisions, and put off legal or money matters until you feel more in control.

Sunday, 4th May

Moon conjunct Saturn

I'm afraid it's a day full of anxiety for you. The Moon has met the grim planet Saturn in your house of image and personality so the whole question of who you are and how you project yourself is uncertain now. It's too easy for you to take the negative view and blame yourself for supposed shortcomings at the moment. You really shouldn't be so hard on yourself. Of course you've got faults, but then again so has everyone else.

Monday, 5th May
Mercury into Aries retrograde

Whenever Mercury is in retrograde motion, life becomes muddled and at the moment, this is exactly what is happening to you. You may find it hard to get your head round all the decisions that you have to make and when you ask others for advice, they either won't want to be bothered with you or they won't have anything useful or interesting to say.

Tuesday, 6th May
New Moon

Today's New Moon shows that your financial affairs have reached a point where you have to make a decision. Do you carry on in the old, and rather dreary ways of making and spending your cash, or will you look at the realities and make sensible decisions? This isn't a time to retreat into dreamland, or to carry on with bad budgeting. Look at your monetary state carefully.

Wednesday, 7th May
Sun trine Mars

It's time you realised that money spent on your health is an investment for the future. If you've been feeling under the weather or just anxious to improve your physique, then it's a good idea to spend some cash to ensure that you get the body beautiful. It may be membership of a health club or a course of vitamins, but however this urge strikes you, it'll be worth it in the long run.

Thursday, 8th May
Mercury direct

At last, Mercury turns tail and starts to move forward, bringing to an end a period of confusion or mental frustration that has had you in its grip for the last two or three weeks. You can embark on serious negotiations with others now if needs be and you can move ahead with all kinds of business matters. Any trips which have been delayed can now be taken and muddles and mishaps will soon be cleared up.

Friday, 9th May
Moon trine Jupiter

Friends, neighbours and colleagues are all in an encouraging mood today. They obviously want the best for you so you'd be letting everyone down if you don't take advantage of the luck that is coming your way.

Saturday, 10th May
Venus into Gemini

If you've got any favours to ask, the passage of Venus into your solar house of persuasion shows that you can use considerable charm and eloquence to win others over to your point of view with no trouble at all. A little flirtation combined with a winning way ensures that you achieve your desires. Your creative talents are boosted too so perhaps you should consider writing down your inspirations now.

Sunday, 11th May
Sun square Jupiter

Don't allow your idealism to get out of control. It is all

very well wanting to help every lame duck or to heal the world, but your purse strings will only stretch so far. You're so full of optimism that you will be tempted to take on tasks that are beyond your capacity physically or financially. Be realistic about what you can and cannot do for yourself and others.

Monday, 12th May
Mercury into Taurus

Mercury's timely re-entry into your financial sector should be a great help to your situation. Your mind will now be clear and you can see all issues from a logical standpoint. Now you'll be able to budget sensibly, pay off outstanding debts and generally make sense of your cashflow. The shrewdness that Mercury brings to bear on your economic life will enable you to control income and expenditure.

Tuesday, 13th May
Uranus retrograde

After a few good days, you can't expect steady progress to go too far. Uranus turns retrograde today and that may give you a momentary doubt about the feasibility of many of your hopes. Friends aren't that helpful just now either, so you have to rely on your own inner reserves of strength for a while. Don't give in to despondency.

Wednesday, 14th May
Venus opposite Pluto

Sometimes it's necessary to stand your ground and speak out for what you believe in. A controversy will provoke you into a spirited declaration today, for Venus is opposed to Pluto, endowing you with stubbornness and deep convictions. Be warned, you are going to meet up with some very fixed opinions now, so don't expect any converts to your point of view.

Thursday, 15th May

Moon square Venus

This looks like a lethargic day for usually active Aries people. It's obvious that you've bitten off far more than you can chew in a work situation and are now suffering the after effects. You won't want to be bothered with anything strenuous today.

Friday, 16th May

Moon conjunct Mars

It's a highly energetic and vital day as the Moon conjuncts Mars. It's fast and furious action all the way but at least you've got the physical strength and tenacity to cope with the pressure. In work, if you can keep your head while all around you are losing theirs you won't be doing too badly at all.

Saturday, 17th May

Venus trine Uranus

Love has no rules so when you hear that someone is very attracted to you, you shouldn't be at all surprised. The only problem now is how are you going to signal back?

Sunday, 18th May

Moon trine Venus

Any problems that have been plaguing your personal relationships will melt away today. They may return at another time but for now, peace and quiet will reign. A female friend will do much to calm you down and to help you to regain your sense of humour and perspective.

Monday, 19th May

Moon trine Jupiter

Put on your dancing shoes, grab your partner and head for the high life tonight. Whatever you do and wherever you go, you are set to become the social sensation of the year. If you are single, then get out and about and see who else is alone and available. If you are married, then look to the future and discuss shared aims and intentions with your partner.

Tuesday, 20th May
Sun trine Neptune

The sun's positive aspect to Neptune gives you the feeling that financial security is not that far away. It's true that fortune smiles on your prospects of worldly wealth, but it's important not to overstate your case or take too much for granted. Effort is still required to make the maximum profit, so don't rest on your laurels just yet.

Wednesday, 21st May
Sun into Gemini

Your curiosity will be massively stimulated from today as the Sun enters the area of learning and communication. Other people's business suddenly becomes your own now. That's not to say that you turn into a busybody overnight, it's just that many will turn to you for some guidance. Affairs in the lives of your brothers, sisters and neighbours have extra importance now.

Thursday, 22nd May
Full Moon

You may have to face the fact that you cannot slope off to distant and romantic shores just now. This doesn't mean that you are forever confined to your home, just that you cannot get away right now. Your mood is not only escapist but also rebellious today! You won't want to have anything to do with people who restrict you or who remind you of your chores and duties, but you simply won't be able to escape them.

Friday, 23rd May

Venus sextile Saturn

It's not a day to encourage the attentions of fickle or frivolous people. You've got far more important things on your mind, and at the moment that means money. Though financially today is lucky, it could do with a small boost. Have a good think now, because you can improve your chances of profit by some sensible forward planning.

Saturday, 24th May

Sun opposite Pluto

It would be wise to keep your plans and opinions under wraps today. Walls have ears, and you could do yourself a grave disservice by revealing all to a potential rival. It's also important to be tactful because an awkward phrase from you could seriously offend someone close and turn a friend into an enemy in five minutes. Take care, Aries.

Sunday, 25th May

Moon square Saturn

The call of duty's very strong today. You'll feel as if you've got a mountain of tasks to complete without having the necessary back-up or time to meet your obligations. Calm down. It's not so difficult if you're methodical. Bit by bit you'll complete everything, much to the wonder of those who dumped the lot in your lap in the first place.

Monday, 26th May

Moon conjunct Neptune

You are in a dreamy phase today, and though others may think that you are shirking, the truth is that you are actually quite inspired. Creative ideas are your forte at the moment.

Tuesday, 27th May

Venus trine Jupiter

Invite all your fine friends to a party today or, if this is too complicated to arrange at short notice, then get together with them in the nearest pub or restaurant and enjoy a gossipy get-together. Convivial conversation surrounds you and the connections you make while socialising could turn out to be useful to you in other ways later on.

Wednesday, 28th May

Venus square Mars

The demands of your working world will be heavy today, and you may feel the effects of stress, possibly in the form of headaches or backache. The harsh aspect between Venus and Mars shows how far you've got to go to make your ideas a reality. This is not a signal to be downhearted, however. Look after your own well-being today and you'll soon be back in fighting form.

Thursday, 29th May

Sun trine Uranus

Don't plan anything today! A friend could come up with a suggestion for an impromptu trip. Accept immediately and don't delay. This is a time for impulse and having fun in the company of people who make you laugh.

Friday, 30th May

Moon square Venus

There are some days when you just want to be left alone with your own thoughts. Unfortunately, your popularity is such that others are anxious for your company. If you really want solitude then you'll have to pretend that you're out. Don't answer the door or the phone. Relax, surround yourself with music and sink back into your favourite chair. Alternatively, a long walk in the fresh air will restore your spirits.

Saturday, 31st May
Moon sextile Uranus

A friend may surprise you by dropping in or by calling you up and suggesting that you join them on some jaunt or other. Your mood is rather detached today and you will be able to ride over any problems that are going on around you without being sucked into them.

June at a Glance

LOVE	♥	♥	♥	♥	
WORK	★	★	★	★	
MONEY	$				
FITNESS	●	●	●		
LUCK	∪	∪	∪		

Sunday, 1st June
Moon sextile Jupiter

Luck comes in many guises today. The lunar aspect to Jupiter puts you in a jovial mood to start with, more confident and outgoing. A friend may come up with a suggestion that you would be wise to follow up.

Monday, 2nd June
Moon square Uranus

Don't give in to a temptation to boast of your wealth or

high-flown monetary plans today. The bigger you build up the picture, the greater will be your embarrassment when it all falls like a house of cards. Remember that you're taking a lot on trust at the moment so don't present a hope as a fact. It's another day to be careful with your cash.

Tuesday, 3rd June
Moon conjunct Mercury

Get your bank statements and cheque books out and work out what you have or have not got in hand for your current expenses. You seem to be in the mood to deal with all those boring financial details and, perhaps, this is no bad thing. After all this book-keeping and secretarial work, why not pour yourself an expensive drink and celebrate being in the black, or commiserate with yourself for being in the red once again!

Wednesday, 4th June
Venus into Cancer

Old scores and family squabbles can now be laid to rest as the passage of Venus into your domestic area signals a time of harmony and contentment. Surround yourself with beauty, both in terms of affection and material possessions. This is a good time to renew a closeness with those you love. Join forces to complete a major project such as redecoration, or even a move of home itself. Be assured that the stars smile on you now.

Thursday, 5th June
New Moon

The New Moon shows a change in your way of thinking. In many ways you'll know that it's time to move on. Perhaps you'll find yourself in a new company, a new home or among a new circle of friends in the near future. Opinions are set to change as you are influenced by more stimulating people. Perhaps you'll consider taking up an educational course of some kind.

Friday, 6th June
Mercury trine Mars

The accent is on the state of your health today, helping you invest some time and effort into improving your general well-being. A more assertive and energetic outlook would do you a lot of good in the workplace and, perhaps more pressingly, in your cashflow too. Keep the pace up for the maximum benefits today.

Saturday, 7th June
Sun sextile Saturn

You'll be in a serious frame of mind today, considering many profound and far-reaching issues. Frivolous people will meet with short shrift if they try to involve you in their antics.

Sunday, 8th June
Mercury into Gemini

Your mind will be going at full speed ahead over the next few weeks and you are bound to come up with some really great new ideas. You will be very busy with the phone ringing off the hook and letters falling into your letter box by the ton. You will find yourself acting as a temporary secretary for a while, even if the only person who makes use of your services is you.

Monday, 9th June
Mercury trine Neptune

A brilliant idea on your part should win you a pat on the back from a person in authority. It may be that you save this person's bacon, and without your brainwave, he or she could get into a lot of trouble. Gratitude should be forthcoming.

Tuesday, 10th June

Jupiter retrograde

Just when everything seems to be going along nicely and all that you want is just within your grasp, Jupiter is throwing a spanner in the works. Don't give up; just sit back for a while and wait for better times to come along. This is not a good time to go into a new venture, especially where money is concerned and, if you can avoid making any complicated journeys over the next few weeks, it might be just as well because delays are pretty certain.

Wednesday, 11th June

Sun trine Jupiter

You feel the need to talk things over with someone who can take an objective view of you and your life today and, fortunately, just the right person will come along. Such a chat will give you an opportunity to sort out your beliefs and to begin to form a new and more rational philosophy of life. The stars are happy to give the green light to your most idealistic schemes and they will add zest and zeal to most of your ideas.

Thursday, 12th June

Mercury trine Uranus

The splendid aspect between rational Mercury and inspired Uranus gives a boost to all your mental processes now. A sudden surprise or some welcome news is on its way. There could be a revolution in your way of thinking as old restrictions are swept away, and you'll be free to pursue your aims. Perhaps electronic wizardry comes into this somewhere, but whatever the case, be prepared to accept the new in your life.

Friday, 13th June

Moon conjunct Mars

If you are looking for love, then your workplace is one place where you may find it. Another potential place would be somewhere to do with health and healing. It would be crazy to expect to meet the love of your life in a hospital waiting room, but funnier things have happened and fate can spring some really strange surprises. If you have all the love you need, then just get your work done!

Saturday, 14th June

Moon trine Uranus

If left to yourself, you'd be quite content to be absorbed in home comforts today. However, you've got some demanding friends about to call who'll take you out of your shell by force if necessary, and show you how to paint the town red. Initial resistance will give way to a party mood as you easily outstrip the most energetic soul with a display of fun-filled vitality.

Sunday, 15th June

Mars trine Neptune

You'll have to use some cunning to get your own way today. The usual Aries approach of 'head down and charge' isn't going to work. You'll have to restrain your impatience and fish a little for information. You should follow any clue that will influence your career progress, but don't reveal your hand.

Monday, 16th June

Moon square Neptune

Your mind is likely to be on romance when it should be on more pressing matters at hand. There's a lot of work to be done today, and with you mooning about, it doesn't look as if it's going to be!

Tuesday, 17th June
Moon trine Venus

Those of you who are in settled relationships will find that your lover is in a caring and loving mood today. He or she will be all too willing to soothe your cares away and make you feel deeply loved and appreciated. You may have good news about a joint financial or a domestic matter now and this will enhance your happy mood. The heart-free will enjoy a peaceful day.

Wednesday, 18th June
Mercury sextile Saturn

Though you'll be full of deep thoughts today, there is no reason to become depressed. I know that you feel that you've got a lot to learn, but you are heading in the right direction. . . . all you really need is patience.

Thursday, 19th June
Mars into Libra

Mars enters your solar house of partnerships today. As you can imagine, forceful, dynamic Mars doesn't quite fit into such a gentle sign so you'll have to take care that you don't stomp on the sensibilities of your partner. Try to be more thoughtful and confine your aggression for business.

Friday, 20th June
Full Moon

Today's Full Moon is a chance to banish confusion concerning your beliefs and value systems. You've become aware of certain contradictions and erroneous assumptions, so it's high time that you thought these through and developed some watertight conclusions. Perhaps you've found that many of the concepts you learned in school are no longer relevant, so do something about it and express your own individuality.

Saturday, 21st June

Sun into Cancer

The home and family become your main interest over the next four weeks as the Sun moves into the most domestic area of your chart from today. Family feuds will now be resolved, and you'll find an increasing contentment in your own surroundings. A haven of peace will be restored in your home. This should also be a period of nostalgia when happy memories come flooding back.

Sunday, 22nd June

Sun square Mars

You may be aware of an uncharacteristic generation gap in your family circle today. Your parents may decide not to get on with your partner or your partner may decide not to get on with the younger members of the family. Tempers could fly and someone could storm out in a huff. It is all a storm in a teacup which will soon be forgotten and, hopefully, forgiven too.

Monday, 23rd June

Mercury into Cancer

The past exerts a powerful influence as Mercury enters the house of heritage. You'll find that things long forgotten will somehow re-enter your life over the next couple of weeks. An interest in your family heritage may develop, or possibly a new-found passion for antiques. Some good, meaningful conversations in the family will prove enlightening.

Tuesday, 24th June

Mercury square Mars

Over-reaction to the slightest hint of a problem could start your week off on a sour note. The trouble is that it takes two to tango, and both you and your partner are quite fraught now. The root problem is a family issue which is difficult to resolve. However, if you won't talk about it reasonably there's very little that can be done.

Wednesday, 25th June

Sun conjunct Mercury

A good chat with a relative could open up possibilities and reveal old secrets today. The Sun meets up with Mercury in your solar house of heritage and family issues so you'll take a great deal of pleasure in the company of those who are close to you. This should also be a time to look to the future. Perhaps a move of home should be considered now.

Thursday, 26th June

Mars sextile Pluto

Impulsive is your middle name today, and so is obsessive! You will feel very restless indeed and will want to be off on your travels immediately. No amount of persuasion will make you calm down. Don't rush about so much, you might do yourself an injury!

Friday, 27th June

Venus opposite Neptune

Diplomacy isn't a concept that often occurs to most Ariens, yet that's what's required today. You need kid gloves to handle colleagues and family members who are troubled. At least you will understand why they're in this state, but will you be able to tread carefully enough? Avoid any tendency to indulge in escapist fantasies now. It's not a time to make far-reaching decisions.

Saturday, 28th June

Venus into Leo

This is a good day to begin new projects and to get great ideas off the ground. Venus is now moving into the area of your chart that is concerned with creativity, so over the next few weeks you can take advantage of this and get involved with some kind of creative process. Venus is concerned with the production of beauty, so utilise this planetary energy to enhance the design of any of your creations now.

Sunday, 29th June

Moon square Venus

The course of true love never did run smoothly and today it will run in every direction but the one you want. If you make a date to meet your loved one, you may find yourself left in the lurch because he or she cannot get away to meet you. Money may be an obstacle to your love at the moment and, although this may sort itself out in time, this knowledge doesn't help the way you feel now.

Monday, 30th June

Moon sextile Mercury

This is an excellent time to invest in property or to take on some kind of extra premises. You may want to enlarge or improve your home, acquire business premises or maybe even rent out to others. Brothers, sisters and neighbours may become involved in your plans.

July at a Glance

LOVE	♥	♥	♥	♥	♥
WORK	★				
MONEY	$				
FITNESS	●	●	●	●	
LUCK	∪	∪	∪	∪	∪

Tuesday, 1st July
Venus trine Pluto

The passionate aspect between Venus, planet of love and the dark planet, Pluto, could do a lot for your sex life. The intensity of this influence can spice up your romantic life no end.

Wednesday, 2nd July
Mercury square Saturn

A stubborn family member simply refuses to see sense today, and could easily drive you to distraction since the answer to all problems is as obvious as the nose on your face. Suggestions coming from you will fall on stony ground and you may well have to admit defeat and wait for your foolish relative to come around in his or her own time.

Thursday, 3rd July
Venus sextile Mars

The week begins on a highly emotional note. With the combination of Venus and Mars, both in houses that relate to partnerships and romance, affairs of the heart are the primary concern now. It's said that the path of true love never runs smoothly, but today the amorous route is calm and full of affection.

Friday, 4th July
New Moon

The New Moon falls in the sphere of home and family today, indicating a need for a change. For some reason you've been dissatisfied with your domestic set-up so you may consider looking at house prices in your own, or indeed another area. You probably feel that you need more space and light in your life that your present home isn't providing. A family member may be considering setting up home for themselves and deserves all the encouragement you can give.

Saturday, 5th July
Venus opposite Uranus

If an amorous encounter is planned, you'd better make room for a particularly insensitive person who won't want to go away, no matter how intimate the occasion. You might even have to be downright rude, since dropping hints won't work.

Sunday, 6th July
Mars trine Uranus

Unexpected events are likely to take you by storm today. Someone you know socially could make a romantic declaration which will take you aback. You may not find this person interesting in that way, but at least you'll be flattered.

Monday, 7th July
Mercury opposite Neptune

It doesn't matter what you have to do or what pressures

are being placed upon you today, because this is one of those days when you simply cannot stir yourself into useful action.

Tuesday, 8th July
Mercury into Leo

Mercury moves into a part of your horoscope that is concerned with creativity. Mercury rules such things as thinking, learning and communications, but it can also be associated with skills and craft work of various kinds. The combination of creativity and craft work suggests that the next few weeks would be a good time to work on hobbies such as dressmaking, carpentry and so on.

Wednesday, 9th July
Mercury trine Pluto

Your mind is restless today, leaping around from one subject to another like a grasshopper. There is a sense of dissatisfaction and boredom with everything that you do, even if it is supposed to be enjoyable.

Thursday, 10th July
Moon trine Neptune

There's a very psychic atmosphere around you today. The mingled influences of the Moon and Neptune make you extremely receptive and intuitive now. You'll be sensitive to the feelings and the motives of those around you.

Friday, 11th July
Sun square Saturn

Pressures from your family weigh heavily on your shoulders today. A lot is expected of you and you may not know which way to turn. Of course you want to please, but when all the desires of those around you are mutually contradictory, what are you to do? Today provides another lesson that sticking firmly to the tried and true does not provide the answer to your quandary. Try not to take things so seriously.

Saturday, 12th July
Moon sextile Venus

A sparkling aspect between the Moon and Venus will make this a most romantic day. If you have been looking for someone to love, you could find the right candidate today. So, whatever your circumstances, try to make this the most pleasant and affectionate of days for you *and* all your loved ones.

Sunday, 13th July
Moon square Neptune

There are too many demands on your time and attention today. Both your partner and your work colleagues will want you to be in two places at once. You can't possibly please everybody, so please yourself!

Monday, 14th July
Jupiter sextile Saturn

Though you may feel rather insecure and unsure of your abilities, it's certain that your friends have a far higher estimation of your talents than you do at the moment. What's more, they're right!

Tuesday, 15th July
Mercury sextile Mars

You'll be a silver-tongued charmer today, with enough sex appeal to drive anyone wild with desire. You can use your seductive wiles to good advantage because no one could possibly resist you.

Wednesday, 16th July
Moon sextile Uranus

Mentally, today gives you a wake-up call. Friends and associates will urge you to get out of the normal rut. Visit somewhere new in the company of like-minded people. Your curiosity and awareness of the spiritual dimension of life is mingled with enjoyment and fun.

Thursday, 17th July
Moon trine Saturn

There are some days when your own desires have to come second because the call of duty is very strong. At least you're in the sort of mood to shoulder responsibility for other people.

Friday, 18th July
Mercury opposite Jupiter

Younger members of the family may be a bit of a pain in the neck today. Children may allow their imaginations to run away with them and you may find yourself committed to a course of action or to a load of unexpected expense as a result. If friends come up with crazy ideas, you don't need to throw cold water on them but, equally, don't become involved in a situation you might later regret.

Saturday, 19th July
Moon square Saturn

Slight problems are forecast on the work front today. Don't over-react to any developments because everything will work out in the end. Older family members may be awkward and require a lot of patience.

Sunday, 20th July
Full Moon

Today's Full Moon shows that important decisions have

to be made at a time of rapidly changing circumstances. News that arrives today could well be disturbing, yet will prove to be a blessing in disguise in the long run. You may be considering a move of home, possibly to a distant location, or even throwing in your present career to take up an educational course of some kind. People you meet while travelling will have important things to say.

Monday, 21st July

Sun opposite Neptune

The Sun opposes Neptune this Monday which doesn't do anything for your self-confidence. You're likely to be prone to vague fears and anxieties now. If you were more logical you'd see that there's very little to be concerned about as long as you aren't gullible. Avoid any glib talkers like the plague.

Tuesday, 22nd July

Sun into Leo

You are going to be in a slightly frivolous frame of mind over the next few weeks and you shouldn't punish yourself for this. Pay attention to an interest or a demanding hobby now or get involved in something creative on behalf of others. A couple of typical examples would be the production of a school play or making preparations for a flower and vegetable show.

Wednesday, 23rd July

Venus into Virgo

Venus moves out of the fun, sun and pleasure area of your chart into the work, duty and health area, and it will stay there for the next few weeks. This suggests that any problems related to work and duty will become easier to handle, and also that you could start to see some kind of practical outcome from all that you have been doing. If you have been off-colour recently, Venus will help you to feel better soon.

Thursday, 24th July
Moon trine Pluto

You're in a forceful and direct mood today. As the Moon contacts Pluto, you're ready, willing and able to stand for a point of principle with a stubbornness that should be a surprise for everyone around you. Anything you feel strongly about will be expounded with a fervour that would put a preacher to shame.

Friday, 25th July
Venus square Pluto

Boring drudgery could get you down today if you let it. Your mind is on distant, exotic shores, certainly not on doing the dishes! Those with dull jobs had better be careful because for two pins you could throw it all in, only to regret your actions later.

Saturday, 26th July
Mars trine Jupiter

Someone who has hitherto been a good friend could now begin to become something much more important to you. You may embark on a business partnership with a pal or, alternatively, you could become aware that your friend feels far more for you than mere friendship. The only thing that is likely to go wrong is that you can take the wrong attitude and spoil everything, so relax. Don't make too much of what others say and enjoy yourself.

Sunday, 27th July
Mercury into Virgo

The movement of Mercury into the sign of Virgo suggests that a slightly more serious phase is on the way. Over the next three weeks or so you will have to concentrate on what needs to be done rather than on having a good time. You may have a fair bit to do with neighbours, colleagues and relatives around your own age group soon, and you will have to spend a fair bit of time on the 'phone to them.

Monday, 28th July
Mars opposite Saturn

The opposition between those two mean planets, Mars and Saturn, spells trouble in a close relationship. Harsh words are likely to be spoken if either or both of you are too headstrong for your own good, and for the good of your partnership.

Tuesday, 29th July
Sun opposite Uranus

The Sun opposes Uranus today which has the effect of an earthquake running through your life. Literally anything could happen in your personal affairs. A sudden infatuation or revolutionary inspiration could set you off in a totally new direction. Of course, Uranian influences don't always have long-term effects so you could find yourself high and dry if you don't think your moves through carefully.

Wednesday, 30th July
Moon trine Mars

Whether you are warming up a new relationship or re-heating an old one, today's excellent aspect between the Moon and Mars will help you to get things going in the right direction. You will be able to get your ideas across to others easily now and they will be happy to act on your behalf if you ask them.

Thursday, 31st July
Moon sextile Mercury

Good news! If you are waiting for something to be fixed at home or at work, it will be. Frustrations will melt away as friends, neighbours and relatives rush round to help out with all those minor chores and problems that are plaguing you. A neighbourhood event may provide some unexpected amusement and pals who pop in may provide some more.

August at a Glance

LOVE	♥				
WORK	★	★			
MONEY	$	$			
FITNESS	●	●	●	●	●
LUCK	∪	∪	∪		

Friday, 1st August
Saturn retrograde

The planet Saturn has cast a cloud over the expression of your personality for some time now, and from today, as the ringed planet halts his forward progress it's a good time to have a good think about your image. Perhaps you've been presenting a far too grim aspect to the world, so try to lighten up. You need to be very sure that you are in a secure position now so checking and double-checking is in order.

Saturday, 2nd August
Moon trine Pluto

Forget your woes and doubts and prepare for a social time to beat the rest. You should go out to enjoy yourself now. Surround yourself with people who make you laugh. This should be a flirtatious day and anything that will boost your ego is a plus just now. You should be with those who are young in body or mind to make you feel youthful and carefree.

Sunday, 3rd August
New Moon

There's a New Moon today casting a glow over your artistic potential. Your talents should shine now, so have some belief in yourself and in what you can offer to the world at large. Of course if art and literature leave you cold, you may be more inclined to an amorous path. Conventional values are not for you now since you're determined to be yourself and to chart your own course. Make time to have fun – you deserve it.

Monday, 4th August
Moon sextile Mars

Stave off the dreaded encroachment of boredom and whisk yourself and your lover off to paint the town red. Your lover will find it hard to keep up with your pace today, but at least he or she won't find you boring. Try taking your loved one off to enjoy a sporting or other outdoor hobby. Singles will find going out and about even more productive because you may discover the love of your life.

Tuesday, 5th August
Moon conjunct Mercury

When the Moon makes contact with Mercury, mental powers are enhanced. You're very astute now especially when you have to deal with any technicalities. If you're dealing with tradesmen such as plumbers, domestic engineers and the like, you're very sharp. Unfortunately, since the solar house of health is also activated, you may be prone to hypochondria today. More realistically, you may even suffer from some allergy or other. If in doubt consult your doctor.

Wednesday, 6th August
Moon conjunct Venus

You can expect women to be a great help to you today and, whether these females be relatives, friends or even new acquaintances, they will do a great deal for you. Your female friends and companions will not only be on hand to give you useful practical help but also to boost your confidence and allow you to talk over a few troublesome problems with them.

Thursday, 7th August
Moon sextile Pluto

Relationships are made up of a lot of ingredients, and the reason that truly successful ones are rare is that in most there's a fundamental lack of understanding between partners. It's important therefore not to assume that you know all there is to know about your other half. You need to confide some of your deepest feelings now. Not just the good ones, but your fears and anxieties too. Only in this way will you achieve the closeness you both desire.

Friday, 8th August
Moon sextile Sun

This is a good time for your love life. If you are deeply committed then you should share quality time with your partner. If single, then today could bring you into contact with someone who will become extremely important romantically.

Saturday, 9th August
Sun opposite Jupiter

You may think that it is not worth holding onto your hopes, wishes and dreams for the future, but this is not the case. You may be suffering from a number of setbacks and there could be one or two real obstacles to your search for happiness. These setbacks and obstacles are purely temporary and there will soon come a time when you can begin to reach out for what you want from life once again.

Sunday, 10th August
Mars square Neptune

Although you're full of good intentions, you're a mite too disorganised to get anything done today. The energy may well be there but your sense of discipline isn't, and perhaps you haven't thought things through too well either.

Monday, 11th August
Moon square Sun

You may still be in the mood for fun and adventure, but those close to home don't appreciate your apparently selfish actions. A money worry may emerge today, which will not encourage harmony. Very little can be resolved now, so wait until this stellar influence passes.

Tuesday, 12th August
Sun trine Saturn

In total contrast to yesterday's frolics, the Sun makes a good aspect to Saturn now which puts you in an extremely practical frame of mind. Any personal or creative venture can be put on a sound footing by your innate common sense. In affairs of the heart, this aspect will clarify exactly what you need out of a relationship.

Wednesday, 13th August
Pluto direct

Pluto returns to the correct path today so you'll get a much-needed glimmer of optimism. You'll gain the sense that there is light at the end of the tunnel, and you could embark on a long-term course, leading you into areas you've never considered. In spiritual, educational and philosophical matters, your horizons are expanding. Dreams take a step nearer to fulfilment.

Thursday, 14th August
Mars into Scorpio

Mars moves into Scorpio today, which heightens your feelings. Your passions will be aroused in some important way and you could find yourself behaving in an unusual manner due to the depth of your emotions. Make sure that you are not simply reacting out of anger or due to some kind of feverish response.

Friday, 15th August
Venus trine Neptune

The dreamy influence continues as Venus makes a positive aspect to Neptune, encouraging you to allow your imagination free rein. You may find work pressures too difficult to bear without the odd day dream. This is an excellent aspect for all those involved with creative work because your talents will shine. However, money matters should be left well alone.

Saturday, 16th August
Venus into Libra

Venus, the planet of romance, moves into your horoscope

area of close relationships from today, increasing your physical desires and bringing the light of love into your heart. If you're involved in a long-term partnership it's a chance to renew the magic of the early days of your union. If single, then the next few weeks should bring a stunning new attraction into your life.

Sunday, 17th August
Mercury retrograde

Everything comes to a dead stop in your working environment as Mercury again pauses in his course. News of opportunities may now be delayed. Letters, phone calls and professional contacts are either mistimed or full of evasion. Don't worry, this period will pass, but you'll have to be patient.

Monday, 18th August
Full Moon

Today's Full Moon could make you feel a bit tetchy and tense and it could also bring you some sort of unexpected expense. The best thing to do today is to stick to your usual routine and not start anything new or important. Jog along as usual and try not to become caught up in anybody else's bad mood now.

Tuesday, 19th August
Moon opposite Mercury

If you are engaged in a long and detailed task such as dressmaking, do-it-yourself or craft works of some other kind, you may find the going difficult today. You could encounter unexpected difficulties in your task or you may have to set the whole job aside in order to do something more important for a while. Work of all kinds could be frustrating for at least part of the day.

Wednesday, 20th August
Moon sextile Neptune
All you need is some peace and quiet to get your thoughts in order. Any outside pressure will be counterproductive because you need some time to yourself and to work at your own pace.

Thursday, 21st August
Venus trine Uranus
Those who are involved in a new relationship should take the opportunity afforded by the aspect between Venus and Uranus to introduce your partner to your friends. This can be a delicate moment, yet you'll find that everyone will be in tune. For those who are already involved in a long-term emotional link, this is a time to involve your partner more in your activities.

Friday, 22nd August
Mars square Uranus
This is a volatile day full of snares for the unwary. If you go with your instincts, you'll ignore all warnings and rush ahead with your ill thought-out plans regardless. You can expect some fierce opposition and possibly an explosion of long-suppressed feelings. Don't touch your cash now, or take friend's words at face value. In fact, take extra care in everything.

Saturday, 23rd August
Sun into Virgo
The Sun moves into your solar sixth house of work and duty for the next month. This solar movement will also encourage you to concentrate on your health and well-being and also that of your family. If you are off-colour, the Sun will help you to get back to full health once again.

If you have jobs that need to be done, the next month or so will be a good time to do them.

Sunday, 24th August
Moon trine Neptune

The idle fantasy of a moment deserves closer attention because it could contain the germ of a business idea that could make you a lot of cash. Dream on, because while you dream you're still working!

Monday, 25th August
Sun square Pluto

The Sun's aspect to Pluto has got hints of guilt and regret. You may be feeling a little under the weather so it wouldn't be a good idea to take on too much just now. Those around you don't seem too sympathetic either, so try to have a quiet day.

Tuesday, 26th August
Moon sextile Saturn

No task is too big or too difficult for you today. Your attention to detail and determination to finish are your best assets. Even if you have a mountain of work to get through, you will accomplish it all with ease.

Wednesday, 27th August
Moon sextile Sun

If you need to get through some chores in and around your home, this is a good day to do so. Do-it-yourself jobs, tidying up, cooking, cleaning and gardening will all go well and make you feel that you have spent the day in a really useful way.

Thursday, 28th August

Venus trine Jupiter

Today has all the appearance of being a real red-letter day because both Venus and Jupiter are throwing a beneficial light on all your schemes. If you have been harbouring secret feelings for that fascinating member of the opposite sex, then today is the day to chance your arm and ask them for a date. If you have a money-making idea on your mind, then give it a go.

Friday, 29th August

Mercury sextile Mars

You're a shrewd operator today. Complex financial affairs can't get the better of you. Neither can officialdom or red tape. You've got the measure of all opposition and have the brain and the brawn to deal with all of it!

Saturday, 30th August

Moon square Mars

It'll be hard to keep anything in perspective at the moment since there's a harsh aspect between the Moon and Mars. Your feelings run high and you could experience emotional highs and lows. You're altogether too sensitive now and will rise to the bait in any conversation that could turn into an argument. If you want a quiet life, then keep your head down for a while.

Sunday, 31st August

Sun conjunct Mercury

You will be a source of wonder today as you effortlessly tackle anything and everything that the world can throw at you. The Sun's conjunction with Mercury puts a powerful emphasis on your house of work so this is the time to improve your prospects and generally make your way up the ladder of success. This is a good day to attend interviews and otherwise get your views and ideas a fair hearing. You can't afford to sit back and wait any longer. Don't hide your light under a bushel.

September at a Glance

LOVE	♥	♥	♥	♥	♥
WORK	★	★	★		
MONEY	$	$			
FITNESS	●	●	●	●	
LUCK	∪				

Monday, 1st September

New Moon eclipse

There is an eclipse today and this means that you will have to face up to the fact that something in your life needs to be changed. The evidence is that you need a change of job but you will need to look at your own personal birth chart in some detail in order to work out whether this is the real reason for your currently unsettled state of mind.

Tuesday, 2nd September

Venus opposite Saturn

The path of true love never runs smoothly, you should know that by now, so when your other half seems strangely despondent, don't be too ready to blame yourself. The chances are that it's nothing to do with you at all. Just be there with lots of sympathy.

Wednesday, 3rd September
Moon trine Neptune
A sudden inspiration could save you a lot of time. Urgent tasks can be speeded up immeasurably. The speed of your intellectual grasp and your instinctive understanding of how to create a shortcut is breathtaking.

Thursday, 4th September
Moon trine Jupiter
Solo Ariens could find the answer to a maiden's prayer today. In short, romance is in the air and you shouldn't turn your back on any chance of finding love. Even if this turns out to be nothing more than a fleeting flirtation, it will do wonders for your ego and it will bring the spring back into your step once again.

Friday, 5th September
Moon conjunct Venus
If you are a man or if you are reading this on behalf of a man, you can expect something very romantic and pleasant to happen. If you happen to be a woman, then you can expect to have some kind of pleasant social event in the company of other women today. All working relationships, partnerships, marriage or other personal relationships will be well starred today.

Saturday, 6th September
Sun sextile Mars
There's a golden opportunity to improve your financial status today. The Sun and Mars are well aspected showing that you can increase your savings, or make an advantageous investment. It would be a good time to resolve some old debts, and to make some regular contributions to a pension fund or other long term scheme. Your sure instincts won't let you down now.

Sunday, 7th September
Mercury square Pluto

After yesterday's high hopes, you're brought back down to earth by the harsh aspect between Mercury and Pluto. A snide person could well put a damper on your plans by pointing out all the objections possible. The trouble is that you're too sensitive to take this sort of thing, but do try to maintain your enthusiasm in the face of opposition.

Monday, 8th September
Moon sextile Neptune

It would be too easy to get carried away with an obsession today, even when there's lots that you could be getting on with. A problem with insurance or an inheritance matter could crop up.

Tuesday, 9th September
Moon sextile Jupiter

Jupiter will stimulate the more idealistic and philosophical side of your nature. Travel is well starred now, as are all contacts with foreign people and ideas. This is also a good time to begin a course of training or education of some kind. In short, do anything that is likely to expand your mental and physical horizons today.

Wednesday, 10th September
Mercury direct

You should feel less on edge and generally more healthy as Mercury gets back into his proper course from today. However, a friend may be applying pressure to get you to do something that you're not at all keen on. Fortunately, Mercury's forward motion should ensure that you have the eloquence to defuse the situation without ruffling any feathers.

Thursday, 11th September
Venus square Neptune

You're a little too self-serving for comfort today. You'll be happy to weave a web of deceit hoping that an unflattering truth won't come to light. You're only deceiving yourself, and it would be better if you just admitted your fault immediately rather than risking the consequences when it gets out later.

Friday, 12th September
Venus into Scorpio

Venus enters the area of your chart that is closely involved with love and sex today. Oddly enough, this aspect can bring the end of a difficult relationship, or just as easily begin a wonderful new one. If you have been dating but haven't yet got around to 'mating', this could be the start of something wonderful. Your emotional life over the next two or three weeks should be something to remember, that's for sure!

Saturday, 13th September
Moon conjunct Uranus

New friends may be unconventional, even eccentric, but you've got to admit that they're entertaining. The company of lively people provides some marvellous stimulation now. A perfect antidote to more mundane work affairs. Give in to temptation now, and seek out novel experiences in new locales. The social scene should be fun filled.

Sunday, 14th September
Moon square Mars

You may be under some economic pressure but some people around you are convinced that you're made of money, and equally keen to spend it. It doesn't matter how much you reasonably protest that you can't really afford too many treats – you won't be believed. It's time to take some radical action and put your foot down firmly. Refuse to part with cash because apart from the financial loss, it'll cause long-term resentment on your part.

Monday, 15th September
Mercury sextile Venus

You will probably have to put yourself out on behalf of others today, but fortunately they will appreciate what you are doing for them and they will return the favour when they can.

Tuesday, 16th September
Full Moon eclipse

Today's eclipse concentrates on your working life and shows you that it may be time to call a halt to any activity that isn't giving you sufficient rewards or satisfaction. If your health's been troubling you then it's time to get the problem sorted out once and for all. Ignoring an ache won't make it go away. If you have any fears on this score then surely it's better to check everything out, if only to set your mind at rest. Perhaps the only true cure to health worries and work concerns is a complete change of routine.

Wednesday, 17th September
Venus square Uranus

No matter how serious your intent either to increase your personal hoard or to indulge in some more intimate pleasures with the one you love, friends or, at least those who call themselves friends, will be a disruptive influence on your plans now. They seem to be making a conscious effort to distract you so you'll have to be firm. The more demanding people get, the harder you should strive to disassociate yourself from such disruptive influences.

Thursday, 18th September
Moon conjunct Saturn

Your mood could be low today, with no obvious reason for a depressive state of mind. We all get days like this so you need to distract yourself with something you enjoy. Go on, smile. You might convince yourself to be happy by the end!

Friday, 19th September
Sun trine Neptune

You are inspired today and your creative approach will impress people of authority. Originality is the key to progress now, and the way you intuitively reach the solution to work problems is a major asset.

Saturday, 20th September
Moon opposite Mars

Financial worries govern the day as the Moon opposes Mars in fiscal areas of your chart. Try not to over react to any minor economic problems. Your temper is frayed but if you are systematic you can sort out monetary problems before they arise.

Sunday, 21st September
Moon opposite Pluto

As much as you try to show others the extent of your feelings, and what you regard as important, friends and colleagues seem too wrapped up in their own concerns to pay you much heed. Even if they did, their reactions would vary between outright mockery and being patronising. You're extra sensitive today so it's a time to keep your head down and your opinions to yourself. You can't expect much understanding when the Moon opposes Pluto.

Monday, 22nd September

Sun into Libra

Today the Sun moves into the area of your chart devoted to relationships. If things have been difficult in a partnership, either personal or in business, then this is your chance to put everything back in its proper place. It's obvious that the significant other in your life deserves respect and affection, and that's just what you're now prepared to give. Teamwork is the key to success over the next month.

Tuesday, 23rd September

Venus square Jupiter

The social side of life could be quite good, but the financial side looks a bit less promising just now. This is not the best time to book an expensive holiday or to agree to do things that are beyond your financial means. A woman may become a financial burden on you and you may have to tell her that you are not interested in carrying her and her problems on your shoulders.

Wednesday, 24th September

Mars sextile Neptune

Sometimes actions speak louder than words, and this is all the more effective when you know that your actions are right! Today, something that has needed to be done will be accomplished. This will be down to your own courage and decisiveness!

Thursday, 25th September

Moon opposite Neptune

A vague and unsettling day when peace is difficult to find and your mind will be prone to vague fears. The last thing you need is to be left alone to ponder, so find some company to soothe your nerves.

Friday, 26th September
Sun sextile Pluto

It is time to take the lead in a relationship. If you are assertive, you can banish all confusions and renew an understanding with your loved one. Your passions are strong factors in this and your partner will see that going along with you is the easiest course.

Saturday, 27th September
Sun trine Uranus

Prepare to be surprised by an expression of character that you'd never expect from someone you thought you knew so well. Everyone's got a few small foibles but this one could really set your mind, and possibly your pulse, racing. Even your partner in life could show a side to his or her nature that's a shock to your system. That should put a smile on your face.

Sunday, 28th September
Mars into Sagittarius

You could find yourself travelling over great distances at some time during the next few weeks. You may be asked to visit friends or family who live overseas now. You may restrict your travelling to mental journeys by taking up a course of study or training.

Monday, 29th September
Void Moon

This is one of those days when none of the planets is making any worthwhile kind of aspect to any of the others. Even the Moon's course is void, which means that it is not making any significant aspects to any of the other planets. On such a day, avoid starting anything new and don't set out to do anything important. Do what needs to be done and take some time off for a rest.

Tuesday, 30th September
Mercury trine Neptune

It's time to stop thinking about your own immediate interests and repay a favour or kindness from the past. Show yourself to be a thoughtful and generous person. Your reputation can only increase by a unselfish action performed now.

October at a Glance

LOVE	♥	♥	♥		
WORK	★	★	★	★	
MONEY	$	$	$		
FITNESS	●				
LUCK	∪				

Wednesday, 1st October
New Moon

The only planetary activity today is a New Moon in your opposite sign. It is possible that this could bring the start of a new relationship for the lonely but, to be honest, this planetary aspect is a bit too weak for such a big event. It is much more likely that you will improve upon a current relationship rather than start a new one at this time.

Thursday, 2nd October
Mercury into Libra

The inquisitive Mercury moves into your solar house of marriage and long-lasting relationships from today, ushering in a period when a renewed understanding can be reached between you and your partner. New relationships can be formed under this influence too, though these will tend to be on a light, fairly superficial level. Good humour and plenty of chat should be a feature for a few weeks, but you must try to curb a tendency to needlessly criticise another's foibles. Remember, not even you are perfect!

Friday, 3rd October
Mercury sextile Mars

If you are in a settled relationship such as marriage, you should try suggesting to your partner that you take a trip or holiday soon. He or she will probably jump at the chance. If you are single, then get yourself involved in any kind of outdoorsy hobby which brings you into contact with interesting people. You are in an adventurous mood and you are quite ready to do anything from riding a camel to bunjee jumping.

Saturday, 4th October
Sun trine Jupiter

Never mind the expense, romance is more important! Take the one who means most to you out for a night on the town. This is a supremely lucky day for you to have a lot of fun and to bask in affection. Your lover will appreciate the treat.

Sunday, 5th October
Mercury trine Uranus

This is a day for inspiration. The planet Mercury, ruler of the mind, is strongly influenced by the lightning flash of brilliant Uranus. No matter what your idea, or what reception you think it'll get from your partner, try it out. You'll probably find that your other half has also been thinking along similar lines, so you're both in tune yet again.

Monday, 6th October
Venus sextile Neptune

Tread carefully today, because the feelings of those around you are too sensitive to be tampered with. You need a lot of tact just to get along now. In both work and family affairs it's like walking on eggshells, yet you'd be well advised to do just that if you want a peaceful life. At least you're in a sympathetic and understanding mood.

Tuesday, 7th October
Venus into Sagittarius

Venus enters Sagittarius today, and this may make you slightly restless. Venus is concerned with the pleasures of life and also with leisure activities of all kinds, so explore such ideas as your sporting interests, listening to music or going to art galleries and the like. You may want to travel somewhere new and stimulating soon.

Wednesday, 8th October
Jupiter direct

You may have felt for much of this year as though you have been walking through treacle, but the movement of Jupiter into direct motion today will free you from these constraints and allow you to get on and do your own thing. There is an air of optimism now which will help you to believe in yourself and begin to make your dreams come true.

Thursday, 9th October
Neptune direct

As the distant planet Neptune resumes its slow, direct course, you'll be reassured that your professional dreams have some chance of fulfilment. You've got a long way to go yet, but you are on the right road. Trust your instincts.

Friday, 10th October
Sun opposite Saturn

It would be too easy for you to become discouraged today. Many tasks seem too enormous to cope with, no matter how hard you try. Even the soothing words of a close friend or partner won't have the desired effect. Try to believe in yourself more.

Saturday, 11th October
Venus conjunct Pluto

When Venus meets Pluto, some uncomfortable emotions rise to the surface. Deep unconscious impulses are about to be faced and, if these involve sexual attraction, they are likely to complicate existing relationships. Pluto is the planet of fate, so what can you do about it?

Sunday, 12th October
Venus sextile Uranus

Today you are a creature of impulse, ready to throw off responsibilities and have fun. We wouldn't be surprised if you soon found yourself in another part of the world, enjoying a flirtatious dalliance before this influence ends.

Monday, 13th October
Sun conjunct Mercury

You and your lover have a great deal to talk over and today is the day to do it. If you are in the early stages of a relationship, you will find that you have a great deal in common and you will be able to while away many happy hours together discussing your childhoods and backgrounds. If you have something that is niggling you,

you should not keep this to yourself because it will linger there, possibly causing long-term resentment.

Tuesday, 14th October

Uranus direct

Uranus starts up a direct motion today. This planetary event should enhance your view of the world, and no matter what your personal hobbyhorse, you'll be left with the idea that improvements are possible. The state of the world won't seem so hopeless from now on. Many of your past efforts will now start to pay off.

Wednesday, 15th October

Mars sextile Jupiter

The pursuit of happiness is all very well, but you need to develop a little wisdom and understanding along the way. Therefore, you could now find yourself thinking over important matters and also taking the trouble to find something out before making any major decisions. You could start a course of training today or you may decide to take lessons which would help you improve in your chosen sport or hobby.

Thursday, 16th October

Full Moon

Today's Full Moon suggests that all is not well with at least one personal relationship. You could find someone close to you acting in a particularly awkward manner now, or you may find that it is impossible for you to get through to them.

Friday, 17th October

Mercury square Neptune

There's not much point in trying to explain your thoughts today. The planet of the mind, Mercury, is hopelessly confused by the vagueness of Neptune and nothing will come out quite as you mean it.

Saturday, 18th October

Venus sextile Jupiter

The two planets of good fortune, Venus and Jupiter, are in harmony today, so if you've been longing to travel you should now find that your wish could come true. All in all an excellent time to plan a holiday.

Sunday, 19th October

Mercury into Scorpio

Mercury moves into one of the most sensitive areas of your chart from today. Anything of an intimate nature, from your physical relationships to the state of your bank balance, comes under scrutiny now. Turn your heightened perceptions to your love life, important partnerships, and any affair that deals with investment, insurance, tax or shared resources. An intelligent approach now will save you a lot of problems later.

Monday, 20th October

Sun square Neptune

You may feel that recent difficulties are now behind you, but you aren't quite out of the woods yet. The Sun's aspect to Neptune shows that self-deception is too easy. Be conscious of the care you have to take both in close relationships and in your career. Don't take anything at face value today.

Tuesday, 21st October

Mars trine Saturn

Nothing should be beyond you now! The strength and determination of Mars matches the staying power of Saturn ensuring that you will be successful in whatever you do. If embarking on a long-term project, you will be sure of success in it!

Wednesday, 22nd October
Mercury square Uranus

News received today is likely to be rather disturbing and it could come out of the blue. The events in a friend's life may give cause for concern, but there is nothing to do but await developments.

Thursday, 23rd October
Sun into Scorpio

Today, the Sun enters your solar eighth house of beginnings and endings. Thus, over the next month, you can expect something to wind its way to a conclusion, while something else starts to take its place. This doesn't seem to signify a major landmark or any really big event in your life, but it does mark one of those small turning points that we all experience from time to time.

Friday, 24th October
Venus trine Saturn

You've been dreaming of far-off lands, and mentally playing with the many diverse aspects of life. Unfortunately you have a life in the here-and-now, and there are plenty of duties and obligations that go along with that. You may feel the need to improve your education and general knowledge. If that's so, today's aspect between Venus and Saturn will reveal some practical steps you can take to make your dreams a reality. Plan carefully now because you'll realise that though it may take a long time, with persistence and patience you can fulfil your desires.

Saturday, 25th October

Venus conjunct Mars

Today's conjunction of Venus and Mars opens your eyes to numerous possibilities both in the romantic sense and on a more cultural level. This aspect is undoubtedly good for all affairs of the heart, especially if you can share your insights with someone special. Art, music and theatre may also capture your interest.

Sunday, 26th October

Moon sextile Mercury

As the Moon contacts Mercury it's time to put your cards on the table. A meeting will work in your favour if you are open and honest in your opinions now. Don't be afraid to stand out from the crowd.

Monday, 27th October

Mercury square Jupiter

Don't believe all that you are told today. Talk things over with friends by all means, but use your own judgement when making decisions rather than blindly acting on their advice. Look through the brochures put out by companies that specialise in financial advice and insurance schemes, but don't jump at the first thing that is offered. Think over your present and future needs carefully before buying any of it.

Tuesday, 28th October

Sun square Uranus

A personal crisis could knock you off balance today. A serious issue, either financial or more intimate, needs immediate attention if you are to salvage something. Don't dally, because a lot depends on your actions!

Wednesday, 29th October

Moon opposite Saturn

All is not well on the emotional front today. The lunar opposition to Saturn casts a rather gloomy cloud over your partnerships, both love links and those of the business variety. Your partner may need cheering up.

Thursday, 30th October

Moon square Neptune

It's not going to be a day for co-operation. Those around you at work and at home seem to have so many of their own cares and concerns that they won't be at all interested in what you think or have to say. Of course, most of their worries are mere fantasy, but they won't want to hear you say that either!

Friday, 31st October

New Moon

Apart from a New Moon today, there are no major planetary happenings. This suggests that you should avoid making major changes in your life just now but make a couple of fresh starts in very minor matters. You may feel like taking your partner to task over their irritating ways, but perhaps today is not the best day for doing this. Wait until Saturday!

November at a Glance

LOVE	♥	♥			
WORK	★	★	★	★	★
MONEY	$	$	$	$	
FITNESS	●	●	●	●	
LUCK	∪	∪	∪	∪	

Saturday, 1st November
Moon conjunct Mercury

A declaration of love is certain today as the Moon conjuncts Mercury in your house of passion. This could be the start of something truly spectacular in your love life. You'll be able to talk freely about your most intimate needs and desires now. There's no room for embarrassment when there's such harmony between two people.

Sunday, 2nd November
Moon sextile Uranus

It's a good thing that you've got broad shoulders, because yet again they're going to come in handy when a friend needs some sympathy. Your caring nature comes into its own now. You don't really have to do anything; just be there to listen.

Monday, 3rd November
Moon trine Saturn

If you've been looking forward to a trip away, the excitement should be reaching fever pitch by now. However, there are still some practical considerations to come first. Have you double-checked everything? Even if you have, go over it once more!

Tuesday, 4th November
Sun square Jupiter

You could find yourself agreeing to some kind of totally impossible task, and all this for very little in the way of thanks. You will have to gather your courage together and simply refuse to do this, otherwise you will not have an ounce of strength or a moment of time left for yourself. Don't allow others to talk you into this against your better nature.

Wednesday, 5th November
Venus into Capricorn

You are moving into a phase where you will be able to take charge of your life and your future. You should try to sort out in your mind exactly which goals you want to reach and what ambitions are worth pursuing because the opportunity to get where you most want to be is coming your way. A woman may be instrumental in helping you reach a position of status or possibly to find love, if that is your goal.

Thursday, 6th November
Moon conjunct Neptune

A sensitive day in which you'll be very aware of the undercurrents going on around you. People, too, will be transparent, especially those with naked ambition.

Friday, 7th November
Mercury into Sagittarius

Mercury enters your solar house of adventure and philosophy from today, which stimulates your curiosity. Everything from international affairs to religious questions will tax your mind. Your desire to travel will be boosted for a few weeks, as indeed will a need to expand your knowledge, perhaps by taking up a course at a local college. Keep an open mind, and allow yourself encounters with new ideas.

Saturday, 8th November
Moon square Mercury

Your emotions will cloud your judgement today and you may act on some kind of silly impulse. Don't worry about this and don't regret it, because your intuitive urge may turn out to be more right than you first judged.

Sunday, 9th November
Mars into Capricorn

It's now time for drive, force and ambition as Mars enters the career area, encouraging you to forge ahead with plans. If you feel you want to take a more independent course, this influence favours those who run their own businesses. You'll be very brash and forthright.

Monday, 10th November
Mercury conjunct Pluto

You may begin to take an interest in astrology now, or it may be the Tarot that grabs your imagination. You are in the mood to escape your usual routines, meeting people from different backgrounds and with different interests from your own.

Tuesday, 11th November
Mercury sextile Uranus

Today should prove that you aren't the shy wallflower you've tended to think you were. Mercury's aspect to Uranus shows that you have an intellectual depth that'd be hard to beat. In any and all conversations and debates you'll eloquently hold forth on a wide range of subjects, impressing friends with the panoramic scope of your knowledge.

Wednesday, 12th November
Moon square Neptune

You could be overly sensitive at the moment and particularly vulnerable to the remarks of those around you. Remember that not all comments are barbed, or indeed aimed at you! However, it might be wise to avoid the brash for today at least.

Thursday, 13th November
Moon trine Venus

Anything connected with your work, ambitions and financial fortunes should go very well indeed today. This is a happy, positive day so you'll be quite content with your lot at the moment. Perhaps you're developing a value system that really gives you inner satisfaction.

Friday, 14th November
Full Moon

Today's Full Moon seems to be highlighting a minor problem in connection with financial matters today. You may have been overspending recently and this could be the cause of your current financial embarrassment, but there does seem to be something deeper to be considered here. Perhaps the firm you work for has a temporary problem or maybe your partner is a bit short of cash just now.

Saturday, 15th November
Jupiter sextile Saturn

An excellent day on which luck will combine with opportunity and your innate practicality to ensure success in whatever you do. The company of an older person will be very stimulating.

Sunday, 16th November
Mercury trine Saturn

Today's aspect between Mercury and Saturn particularly favours students and those who are travelling far from home. As far as educational matters are concerned, your intellectual capability and powers of concentration will be enhanced by today's planets.

Monday, 17th November
Mercury sextile Jupiter

You may become a temporary culture-vulture today because your mind is instinctively being drawn to higher things. You may find yourself in a fascinating discussion with interesting people or you may be provoked into deep thought by something that you read. This is a great time for any kind of cultural event or to begin a course of education or training.

Tuesday, 18th November
Uranus sextile Pluto

Very restless urges will set your feet tapping today, and indeed into the immediate future. This rare aspect between Pluto and Uranus gives you a yearning for the different, which could be expressed as a desire for travel or for novelty.

Wednesday, 19th November
Sun sextile Neptune

You are willing to compromise sometimes, but when a work colleague suggests a scheme that doesn't go along with your personal ethics, you will not bend. This is the right course, because your high-minded attitude will win through in business ventures while other shadier deals will not take place.

Thursday, 20th November

Venus square Saturn

The awkward attitudes of a woman could make you fume today. However, this is not the way to win! You need to charm your opponent, even though you'll be doing so through clenched teeth.

Friday, 21st November

Moon square Sun

You need a day of peace and quiet to gather your thoughts. Although friends and family are dear to you, you'd far rather they left you alone just now. Unfortunately some people don't seem to get the message. They're only trying to help, so don't fly off the handle. Explain your desire for solitude clearly, leaving no room for argument. Harmony will be restored.

Saturday, 22nd November

Sun into Sagittarius

The Sun moves into your solar ninth house today and it will stay there for a month. This is a good time to travel overseas or to explore new neighbourhoods. It is also a good time to take up an interest in spiritual matters. You may find yourself keen to read about religious or philosophical subjects or even to explore the world of psychic healing.

Sunday, 23rd November

Moon trine Venus

You've got to be kind to yourself now, because some of the over indulgence of the past few days is beginning to tell on your system. Physically, you need some pampering.

A nice long bath will work wonders for your sense of well-being. This is not a day to overload your work schedule, so take it easy and think up a few treats.

Monday, 24th November
Moon sextile Sun

You feel centred, happy and at peace with the world today and other people are as happy with you as you are with yourself. This is an excellent time to speak with in-laws and other relatives by marriage because they will be able to understand your point of view.

Tuesday, 25th November
Moon square Mars

It looks as though the main thrust of your life is directed toward the achievement of your ambitions today. The only problem with this is that you could ignore the feelings of your partner in life. You've got to balance your time and attention to ensure that your other half doesn't feel neglected. If you set a sensible schedule with a firm cut-off point, you'll have the time you need to renew a romantic acquaintance with someone who means the world to you.

Wednesday, 26th November
Mars square Saturn

Some days it doesn't seem worth getting out of bed, and I'm afraid that this is one of them! The harsh aspect between Mars and Saturn spells out a difficult time in which even simple issues could become a battle! Rest and relax if you can.

Thursday, 27th November
Sun conjunct Pluto

Intellectually, you are on top form today, but a person who thinks that he knows best will irritate you beyond belief.

The problem here is one of ego. He feels insecure and therefore has to prove his superiority. This could become a never-ending battle of wills.

Friday, 28th November

Sun sextile Uranus

Today brings something you've been longing for, and that's a complete change. When the Sun and Uranus mingle their rays, anything can happen, and this time it's all for the good. It's a totally unpredictable planetary influence but there's nothing to be afraid of for all that. All you have to be is open-minded to the new. In fact, you're likely to be ecstatic with joy by the time this day ends!

Saturday, 29th November

Moon conjunct Pluto

This is a far more thoughtful day when you'll delve into memories and reassess many of the pivotal events in your life. You're looking for some level of meaning now, and you'll examine your past to look for a pattern of some sort. You may be faced with major changes again, so it's important to search for clues to help you deal with it in these new circumstances.

Sunday, 30th November

New Moon

The New Moon in your house of adventure urges you to push ahead with new projects. You're in a self-confident mood, and feel able to tackle anything the world throws at you. There's a lure of the exotic today as well, as far-off places exert a powerful attraction. Think again about widening your personal horizons, by travel or by taking up an educational course. You're feeling mentally alert and your curiosity is boundless.

December at a Glance

LOVE	♥	♥			
WORK	★	★	★	★	★
MONEY	$	$	$	$	$
FITNESS	●	●			
LUCK	U	U	U	U	

Monday, 1st December

Moon conjunct Mercury

You can push through a number of career aims today if you want to. Alternatively, you can make real progress in a political or a group activity, as long as this involves money and, better still, has some chance of enhancing your status. If you have something on your mind, it is worth speaking out about it today. If you need a more discreet word in someone's ear, then take them aside and talk to them about your worries.

Tuesday, 2nd December

Moon square Saturn

People in authority aren't in the most sympathetic of moods today, so you'd be wise to steer clear of them. Any confrontation will end with you as the loser, so keep your head down and attend only to your own affairs.

Wednesday, 3rd December

Moon conjunct Venus

The Moon's conjunction with Venus ensures an atmosphere of affection today. I'm sure you'll admit that a little understanding goes a long way so it's important that you make time to show that you care now. If a colleague or working acquaintance is in need of sympathy then make sure that you supply it. You never know, it could do your prospects some good.

Thursday, 4th December
Sun trine Saturn

Long-term projects get a step nearer to a successful completion today, and that fact will do your ego a lot of good. You'll now remember how nervous you once were and realise that you had it in you all the time.

Friday, 5th December
Moon conjunct

Jupiter Today should bring a touch of stardust into your life. You may win something in a raffle or receive a windfall. You will find yourself on the receiving end of karmic debts, suggesting that any money that you may have lent is on its way back to you now, but also that any favours you have done for others will be returned today. Friends will pop in and make you laugh now too.

Saturday, 6th December
Venus conjunct Neptune

Although your ambitions are still occupying your thoughts, the conjunction of Venus and Neptune makes this a sensitive, often sentimental day. Music will have a profound effect on your mood. You need emotional reassurance now, but that's all right because this conjunction stimulates affection too.

Sunday, 7th December
Mercury retrograde

The fact that Mercury goes retrograde today throws a lot

of your financial planning into confusion, and may even bring a note of embarrassment into a close relationship. There's obviously a topic which you feel is impossible to approach now. At least this slow period will give you the chance to reassess both your sexual desires and the prospects of your financial fortunes. If things are going at a snail's pace, you shouldn't be discouraged . . . it's for a good reason. One word of warning: try not to enter any hire purchase or other credit agreements until the middle of next month at the earliest.

Monday, 8th December
Moon square Mercury

There are times when discretion is the better part of valour. You may know something that others don't – in professional affairs especially – so keep your opinions and knowledge to yourself. Indiscretion now will cost you dearly, so if you doubt anyone's reliability, keep silent.

Tuesday, 9th December
Sun sextile Jupiter

You'll be gripped with wanderlust today. Restless urges compel you to leave your usual haunt and seek out adventure. Intellectually, you'll be raring to go with no patience for boring, familiar routines. You want to be up and away – so what's stopping you?

Wednesday, 10th December
Moon trine Mercury

The lunar aspect to Mercury makes your mind extremely perceptive. Any secrets around you will be a secret no longer, for you'll see through any deceit with little trouble. This should be an inspired day which brings out inner abilities that you didn't know existed. Financially too, your luck's in.

Thursday, 11th December
Moon square Jupiter

You may need money to get a project off the ground now and this is a good time to start looking for it. You won't get immediate results from this, but you should keep plugging away until you get the breakthrough that you need. Don't borrow money for unnecessary fripperies but use your credit cards and your borrowing facility wisely.

Friday, 12th December
Venus into Aquarius

Social life, friendships and a general sense of optimism and wonder are due today as Venus enters your solar house of hope and platonic affection. For the next few weeks there will be an ease and understanding with those you deal with. Friends will provide the reassurance and affection that you need at the moment. Your own personal charm too is on a high, while women in your life take on a more important role.

Saturday, 13th December
Mercury into Sagittarius

You should take every opportunity that you can to gather facts, information, impressions and evidence today before going ahead with anything. You may have to deal with legal or official matters now and, if so, having all the right information to hand can only help. If there is nothing specific that you have to deal with, then just keep yourself informed of what is going on in your neighbourhood.

Sunday, 14th December
Full Moon

This is likely to be a really awkward day for any kind of travelling that you have to do. A vehicle could let you down just when you most need it or the public transport that you usually rely upon could suddenly disappear from the face of the earth.

Monday, 15th December
Mars conjunct Neptune

You may know exactly what you want to do, but does anybody else? You may not have explained things clearly enough to those who matter, or maybe you are being particularly slow in picking up what someone else is trying to tell you. Maybe the messages are too subtle for anyone to understand.

Tuesday, 16th December
Saturn direct

Much of the negative thinking that you have been prone to lately will vanish today. Saturn returns to direct motion today, and in doing so allows you to take a more optimistic view of life once again.

Wednesday, 17th December
Sun conjunct Mercury

If you have any kind of legal or official matter to deal with, this is a good day to get on with it. It's a favourable time to sign contracts or agreements or to make a business deal. You seem to be taking a deep interest in spiritual matters now, and this may be the start of something which will affect the course of your life from now on.

Thursday, 18th December
Mars into Aquarius

Friends are likely to be a strong influence on you at this time. Old friends may have interesting ideas to put your way, while new ones could come crowding into your life quite quickly now. You may join some kind of very active group who share your interests and are keen to have you as part of their organisation. This may have something to do with sports or some other kind of energetic or outdoor activity.

Friday, 19th December
Moon square Pluto

You may feel the urge to alter your diet and take a more healthy attitude to your body today. However, any drastic fitness regime or sudden change in your food is likely to do more harm than good. Rome wasn't built in a day, so content yourself with moderate exercise and a sensible intake of nutrition. It's far better than taking up some fad which could upset your system.

Saturday, 20th December
Mercury sextile Jupiter

Forget all the striving and effort today and take some time off to be with your friends. Don't sit around the house dreaming of better things, get down to your local hostelry and see who is about. This will result in interesting conversations and, possibly, even useful contacts for your future development. If you don't belong to any kind of club or society now, consider joining one.

Sunday, 21st December
Sun into Capricorn

The Sun moves decisively into your horoscope area of ambition from today, bringing in a month when your worldly progress will achieve absolute priority. You need to feel that what you are doing is worthwhile and has more meaning than simply paying the bills. You may feel the urge to change you career, to make a long-term commitment to a worthwhile cause, or simply to demand recognition for past efforts. However this ambitious phase is manifested, you can be sure that your prospects are considerably boosted from now on.

Monday, 22nd December
Venus conjunct Mars

A highly active and enjoyable outlook for today. Venus conjuncts Mars in the most social area of your chart so you are bound to be much in demand by all who know you. New friends too are coming into your life, and if your luck's really in, a touch of romance too!

Tuesday, 23rd December
Moon trine Jupiter

It's party time! Let your hair down, head for the nearest pub, club or celebration and have a great outing with your friends. Everyone you meet should be in excellent spirits, so there will be lots of fun on offer.

Wednesday, 24th December
Moon sextile Sun

Even though it's Christmas Eve, your mind will stray back to more material matters for a while today. New work prospects are in the offing. Changes in your career will benefit you ultimately, and you could end up making a considerable profit in the near future.

Thursday, 25th December
Moon square Jupiter

It's a day for putting a brave face on a minor disappointment. All will be well as long as you don't make a mountain out of a molehill when things don't go exactly as you want. After all, it is Christmas Day!

Friday, 26th December

Venus retrograde

There could be a falling out between you and a friend this Boxing Day as the result of Venus's backwards dance. This need not be serious, but quite honestly, the disagreement is totally dependent on how stubborn you are!

Saturday, 27th December

Mercury direct

Mercury resumes a direct course from today which should relieve a lot of the pressures that have been troubling you. Dealing with forms, documents and indeed awkward people should become easier. You'll feel far less intimidated than you have been recently. Your mind is clearer as you'll be more efficient and incisive.

Sunday, 28th December

Mars conjunct Uranus

Anything could happen! The most active planet in the sky, Mars, unites with the unpredictable Uranus, ensuring that whatever does occur, it won't be boring! A surprise party perhaps, or a sudden announcement by a friend about a new romance?

Monday, 29th December

New Moon

Apart from a New Moon today, there is not much going on in the planetary firmament. Take it as easily as you can today, stick more or less to your usual routine and, if you do try something new, make sure that it is nothing large or important. A woman may be instrumental in helping you achieve an ambition and you should be grateful to her for her efforts on your behalf.

Tuesday, 30th December

Moon conjunct Neptune

A day of deep sensitivities is forecast when the Moon unites with the impressionable planet Neptune. It's certain that you will be strongly affected by the moods and feelings of those around you, so make sure that you spend time with people who are happy with a positive view of the world. Avoid the miserable!

Wednesday, 31st December

Moon conjunct Venus

Be sociable and get into the party atmosphere, because you will get much more out of meeting people than you had bargained for. You will make new friends and be filled with new and exciting ideas. It is possible that you will begin to realise that someone whom you had hitherto considered as nothing more than a friend is rapidly turning into someone special. Happy New Year!

Of further interest

ASTROLOGY FOR LOVERS

The Classic Guide to Love and Relationships

Liz Greene

This comprehensive guide to life, relationships and lovers provides an accessible and readable introduction to astrology.

Liz Greene, from her standpoint as trained psychotherapist and astrologer, explains the principles of astrology, debunks popular myths and shows how an understanding of the subject helps in forming lasting relationships.

Included are:

- the personality of each astrological sign
- an explanation of the shadow side
- the difference between the male and female of each sign
- how each sign behaves in love and out of love
- a quick guide to working out your ascendant sign.

UNDERSTANDING ASTROLOGY

A Practical Guide to the Stars

Sasha Fenton

Understanding Astrology provides a concise introduction to this ancient art, showing how it can be used to assess a person's character.

This book takes you beyond the person's 'sun sign' and shows you how to read birth charts. Every element of the horoscope is discussed in simple summaries, along with instructions on how to construct a chart for yourself.

Complete with sample birth charts and astrological tables, this book serves as an ideal starting point for anyone taking their first steps in the fascinating study of astrology.